The Book of Cernunnos

The Book of Cernunnos

Edited by John Beckett & Jason Mankey

ADF
publishing

Published in 2023 by Ár nDraíocht Féin, Shorewood 60404

© 2023 by Ár nDraíocht Féin (First Edition, English)

ISBN 978-0-9889009-7-4 (Paperback)

This book is dedicated to Cernunnos: Lord of the Animals, Lord of the Hunt, and God of the Wild. Because of you, we have stories to tell – and so much more. This book is written and published in your honor.

hail Cernunnos!

Contents

Part 3: Experiencing Cernunnos

Part 4: Poetry

Part 5: Rituals

Epilogue

Introduction

Who is Cernunnos? For some, he is the Horned God of Wicca. For others, he is the Lord of the Animals and the Lord of the Hunt. Still others see him as a God of Liminality and of the Underworld.

Yet for all our ideas about him and experiences of him, we know very little about Cernunnos. His name is recorded only once, on the Pillar of the Boatman, a Latin and Gaulish sculpture near Paris that dates to the early first century CE. Many of us believe it is Cernunnos who is depicted on the Gundestrup Cauldron, but we have no way to know for sure.

This lack of history and lore has done nothing to keep Cernunnos from becoming one of the most popular deities in modern Paganism. It is time he has his own devotional anthology.

This book is the work of 33 writers, artists, and poets. It is our understanding of Cernunnos, our experiences of Cernunnos, and our devotion to Cernunnos. All of them are authentic and none of them are "right" – Cernunnos appears to different people in different ways for different reasons. Perhaps this book will inspire you to seek him out. Perhaps it will help you identify the source of experiences you've already had. Or perhaps it will simply help you to better understand this mighty God and those who follow him.

This is the Book of Cernunnos.

Part 1

history and Theology

Cernunnos Then and Now
Jason Mankey

Then

On September 7, 2016 I visited the National Museum of Scotland in order to view a traveling exhibit there on the people we know today as the Celts. Imaginatively titled *The Celts*, the whole exhibit was interesting but I was really only there to see one specific artifact: the Gundestrup Cauldron.

Most of the time the Gundestrup Cauldron resides at the National Museum of Denmark in Copenhagen, but it spent much of 2016 in the U.K., at the British National Museum and the Museum of Scotland respectively. My trip to Edinburgh in September was planned around two things: whisky and seeing the Cauldron (and not in that order). To me it's one of the most precious and important pieces of art in human history, and that's because the Gundestrup Cauldron is home to the most striking and complete ancient image of the god we call Cernunnos.

The Gundestrup Cauldron would be remarkable even if it lacked Cernunnos. Found in a peat bog in Denmark, the bowl itself is a synthesis of several different cultures. Most likely manufactured near Thrace (near the border of modern Turkey and Greece), the Gundestrup Cauldron contains scenes that are strikingly Celtic. Others are from the Middle East and as far afield as India. The animals depicted in various spots on the Cauldron come from all over Eurasia and are not limited to Europe. It's likely that the Cauldron was used by a Celtic tribe, but just why it's so "worldly" is an open question.

When I saw the Cauldron, it was placed directly in the middle of *The Celts* exhibit. While my wife and I were touring the exhibit it nearly called out to me. I could feel its presence, no doubt amplified by my decades long desire to see it with my own eyes. It's far larger than most people realize, and the famous panels on it look like they were designed to be removed (they appear "clipped" on). The bottom part of the Cauldron was the "working bowl" portion and where the "magick" probably took place. Pictures of the Cauldron reveal the embossed 3-D nature of the artwork (created by hammering images into the back of cauldron's panels), but don't do it justice. I was amazed at just how strongly the images of animals and deities pop out of the Cauldron's silver plates.

The plate depicting Cernunnos is on the inside of the Cauldron and is remarkably different from the other deity images on it. The other deities on the Cauldron all appear larger than life, like giants, and are shown holding human beings in their hands and wrestling with serpents and other mythological creatures. Cernunnos on the other hand appears as a person of regular size, not much larger than the animals which surround him on the Cauldron.

Cernunnos is undoubtedly one of the most popular gods in all of Modern Paganism. Romanticized versions of his image have become the de facto version of the "Horned God" archetype, and his devotees are legion. It's worth pointing out that technically speaking, Cernunnos is not a horned god. There are antlers on the top of his head, and antlers are very different than horns. Antlers are shed annually while horns reside on top of an animal's head for life. There's also nothing linking Cernunnos to fertility either, and the occasional images of Cernunnos with an erect phallus are modern interpretations, not related in any way to how the god was seen in the Ancient World.

Writing about Cernunnos is challenging because we know so very little about him. We have pictures and statues of Cernunnos from antiquity, but what we don't have are mythologies. Cernunnos is a god without a story. A few figures from Irish and Celtic mythology are sometimes linked to the god, but I find most of those arguments extremely speculative at best, and mostly unconvincing. All that we know for certain about his worship in the ancient world comes from the images we have of him. From those we can infer certain things, but even then, there's nothing that can be known with absolute certainty.

There are some scholars who argue that Cernunnos is not even a god, they say that perhaps he was just a well-known chieftain or warrior. Their case is bolstered in some ways by his very lack of name. The word Cernunnos appears only once (and even then without the "C") in antiquity, on a stone pillar found at the present day spot of the Cathedral of Notre Dame in Paris France. That pillar, known as the Pillar of the Boatmen, contains the very recognizable head of Cernunnos, and it's similar to the image on the Gundestrup Cauldron, containing both antlers and torcs. Cernunnos shares the Pillar of the Boatmen with several Roman gods as well as Gaulish-Celtic ones, I think it's great to see him standing so close to Jupiter and Vulcan. The pillar dates to about the first century CE.

There are other ancient artifacts with a name that was probably meant to be Cernunnos. Two metal plaques found in Luxembourg bear the name Cerunincos, most likely in reference to either Cernunnos or a deity like him. A Gaulish inscription found in Southern France, and written in Greek, has also been found that uses the name Carnonos. After that the written record stops, and there's no general consensus on what Cernunnos means in Gaulish.

To figure out who Cernunnos was to his ancient devotees we are left with using his depictions as a guidebook. Depictions of Cernunnos are remarkably consistent and generally contain a combination of the following things:

1. Antlers. Most statues and drawings of the god have antlers. Even the ones that no longer have them may have had them in the past. Several Cernunnos statues had spots for removable antlers, perhaps his antlers were changed depending on the season?

2. Torcs. Cernunnos is almost always depicted with a torc. Sometimes he's holding one, and sometimes he's wearing one. Torcs were a symbol of wealth, power, and nobility in ancient Gaul. From this we can conclude that Cernunnos was associated with those things.

3. Sitting position. Cernunnos is the rare god who is generally depicted sitting. Even when in proximity to other standing deities he still sits. This is often linked to the lotus position of India, and it's certainly possible. But a more likely explanation is that Cernunnos is sitting is a Gaulish hunting posture, or the people of Gaul just preferred to sit on the ground with their legs crossed.

4. Snakes. Cernunnos often carries snakes in ancient art. Snakes are sometimes linked to prophecy, and in some Celtic myths snakes were said to guard hidden treasure.

5. Coins. Piles of gold coins are often shown in proximity to Cernunnos, and oftentimes he seems to be pouring them onto the ground. Metal also comes from the ground, perhaps linking Cernunnos with lands of the dead.

These five attributes are common enough that I think it lays to rest the idea that Cernunnos was a mortal person and not a deity. Though generally confined to Gaul, images of Cernunnos can also be found on the Iberian Peninsula, and possibly in the British Isles (there is a lot of disagreement on whether the figures found there are actually Cernunnos). There are currently less than sixty images/statues that most scholars would say are definitively Cernunnos.

The Gundestrup Cauldron features four of the most common Cernunnos motifs, and does so without any reservations. While some scholars call the image on the Cauldron "the antlered figure" I think it's safe to just call it what it truly is, Cernunnos. On the Gundestrup Cauldron his sitting posture immediately catches the eye, and he both wears and holds a torc. In his right hand is a serpent, and he sits surrounded by animals. Who else could this be but Cernunnos?

From the images of Cernunnos we can infer a few things about he was seen and worshipped in the ancient world:

1. He was a god of hunting. This can be inferred by both the hunting posture and the game animals seen around Cernunnos on the Gundestrup Cauldron. His antlers also suggest a strong link to the natural world. While the Pagan world often tends to look down on personal gnosis, in my own experience he's come to me as a god of the hunt. I'm not alone in this either.

2. He was a god of wealth. We don't tend to think of "horned gods" as money gods, but Cernunnos clearly was. The torcs emphasize wealth, and the depictions of Cernunnos with coinage only confirm this interpretation. Snakes and their association with treasure are another indication of this.

3. He could have been associated with death in some way. Hunting involves death, but there are other links. Detachable horns on some statues suggest that Cernunnos was linked to what we now call the Wheel of the Year in some way. A de-antlered Cernunnos could have represented a fallen deity, or one that simply reflects the annual cycles of birth and death in nature.

On the Reims Stella (found in modern day Reims in France) Cernunnos is shown sitting on a throne in a temple and flanked by the Roman deities Mercury and Apollo. Mercury guided the souls of the dead to the afterlife, could Mercury's proximity to Cernunnos be related to both gods having a role to play in the afterlife? (Mercury was also a god of wealth and commerce, which is another explanation for standing next to Cernunnos.) Even more important than Cernunnos standing next to Mercury is the presence of a rat on the temple's roof, in the ancient world rats were a symbol of the underworld.

Cernunnos can also be linked to boats and bodies of water, both of which were entryways to the Celtic land of the dead. The Pillar of the

Boatmen was paid for by sailors who travelled the River Seine. The panel featuring Cernunnos on the Gundestrup Cauldron contains a woman riding either a dolphin or a large fish, another curious link to Cernunnos and water. Coins, which are mined from the earth and often guarded by gods of death such as Hades, were sacred to Cernunnos, perhaps also linking him to the underworld.

Apart from these three attributes, there's not much else that can be definitively said about Cernunnos's worship in the ancient world. It's certainly possible that he was a god of "other things" but currently we have no way of knowing for sure. Perhaps just as important as Cernunnos's worship in the ancient world as how many of us honor the god today.

Now

The first time I truly experienced Cernunnos was at the Samhain ritual of a friend a little over fifteen years ago. As someone with a reputation for being funny she originally asked me to do something light-hearted for our cakes and ale rite, but I told her I'd prefer something a little more serious. She responded by telling me that I would then instead be drawing down the God of Death and helping to bridge the space between the worlds of the living and the dead.

I prepared for that ritual by reading all that I could on gods of death, knowing that my two usual "go to" deities (Pan and Dionysus) were probably not going to be much help with this particular endeavor. Eventually I graduated from reading to actively seeking out several gods I felt may be of assistance, but my calls to them seemed to fall on deaf ears. No relationships developed, and no presences were detected.

On the night of the ritual I prepared for failure. I had very little confidence that I would be able to do what was required of me. And then once the ritual started, I felt a strong hand on my shoulder, literally guiding me throughout the ritual. I remember looking into the eyes of friends as the Lord of Death and speaking to them, but it was not my voice speaking back. Instead it was the voice of the god who had been guiding me throughout the ritual, Cernunnos.

Eventually I came to know Cernunnos as the Dread Lord of Shadows, a god of both the living and the dead. I feel as if some of this is backed up by what little we know of the god from the ancient past. A hunter is both a dealer of death, but also a preserver of life; they kill so that they and others may live. For me Cernunnos is not bound to one world, he roams wherever He wills, with the souls of those we've lost and the souls of those who reside here.

As a popular "horned god" Cernunnos is most often thought of as a "nature" or "fertility" deity, and I've certainly experienced some of those characteristics. Cernunnos's association with coins suggests an affinity or appreciation for civilization, but for many of us his call is most clearly heard amongst the trees of the wood. It's there surrounded by oaks and firs that I feel him most acutely. Judging by the stories in this book, others feel the same way too.

In the ancient world Cernunnos was never depicted in a sexual manner, and I find myself bothered by overly sexualized modern imagery of the god today, but I still think there's something to Him as a "fertility" deity. When is all right with the natural world, it teems with life, a gift of the earth's fertility. As a lover of the wild spaces it makes sense for Cernunnos to have a vested interest in the continued health and well-being of the natural world.

A few weeks after my initial experience with Cernunnos as a god of death, I met him again on a crisp November night. My wife and I were traveling home from a social engagement when I asked her to stop the car and go on a walk with me through the woods. She was not particularly enthused by the idea but agreed. As we stepped into the woods what little moonlight there was in the sky was immediately blotted out by the trees around us. With some trepidation we carried on, and then heard the sound of rutting deer all around us.

The grunts of the deer were loud and aggressive, and rutting deer do not make for the best of companions. My wife immediately wanted to head back to the car, but I lingered for a moment, feeling energy equivalent to what I had felt at Samhain a few weeks prior. This too was Cernunnos, though the god was in a very different guise.

It's become cliché in the Pagan and Polytheist communities to speak of the gods as having "agency," but I believe their actions and energies influence both us and the world we live in. While it's true that worship or veneration of Cernunnos most likely satisfies some sort of need within us, I believe His presence in the here and now also serves a greater purpose. With the Earth on the brink of ecological disaster I don't think it's a coincidence that worship of Cernunnos has begun anew. I think that He has returned to us to increase our connection to the natural world before it's too late.

Personal gnosis is often frowned upon in the Pagan world. Direct experience with deities are encouraged but is often thought to only matter to the individual who experienced it. This is not the case with Cernunnos. Lacking mythology, personal gnosis has played an outsize role in his modern worship. Most stories involving personal gnosis reveal gods who vary greatly from individual to individual, but in my experience that has not been the case with Cernunnos. Nearly everyone I know who has had some sort of meaningful interaction with the antlered one has had some sort of experience similar to one of my own.

When John and I talk to each other about Cernunnos, we are not recounting stories about three vastly different gods who share a name. Instead we are all speaking about CERNUNNOS. John's experiences with the god have been different from my own but are still clearly experiences with the same deity. At a Druid festival we took part in a Cernunnos ritual written by John celebrating the wilder aspects of the god. At one point in the ritual "John" let out a hearty laugh and gave me a familiar look, but the laugh and the look were not from John, instead they both came from Cernunnos. I know the look and the laugh of an old friend, whether god or mortal.

On Gwion Raven's back there is a striking tattoo of Cernunnos. It's not Cernunnos as he appears on the Gundestrup Cauldron, but Cernunnos as the Dread Lord of Shadows. His face is the skull of a stag and the serpent in His hand and coiling around His body speaks of the mysteries that lie between the worlds. This is also the god whose hand rests on my shoulder at Samhain.

Cernunnos is alive in the world today, and important to tens of thousands of Witches, Druids, and Pagans. He is a friend, a helper, and an ally. His statues adorn our altars and shrines and his name falls happily from our lips. We walk with Him and He walks with us.

hail Cernunnos.

The Rebirth of Cernunnos: Cernunnos as the Pagan Horned God
Jason Mankey

Within much of Modern Paganism the most common male deity is known as "The Horned God." Often thought of as ancient being, today's Horned God is a modern construct, borrowing from literary and historical sources. Most certainly there were horned and antlered deities in the Ancient World, but the differences among those beings were vast. They were also generally unrelated. The Greek god Pan for instance shares absolutely no similarities with Cernunnos (antlers are not horns, and Cernunnos was never depicted with an erect phallus) and yet both of them are thought of as "aspects" of the greater Horned God.

Much of the language used in Modern Paganism to describe the Horned God comes from 19th century depictions of Pan in poetry and prose. There Pan is written about as "the god" of wild spaces, the eternal Lord of the endless and joyous Summer. This way of looking at Pan is not an accurate depiction of his role in Greek mythology. Instead it was a then-modern gloss on the god, and an attempt to use him as a conduit for connection with the natural world.

In addition to Pan as a benevolent earth deity, he was also depicted as a god of sexuality. Not only is Pan mostly attractive to onlookers in poems, he's also often actively copulating with those around him, and often the author. This depiction of Pan is far more accurate than the earlier one, though Pan was rarely thought of as attractive in the Ancient World. Today the modern Horned God construct retains the characteristics once used to describe Pan, but he generally doesn't look like Pan. Instead, he most clearly resembles Cernunnos.

Do a Google Image Search of "Horned God" and you'll end up seeing lots of figures that generally resemble Cernunnos. The horns atop this figure's head are usually not horns at all, but the antlers of a stag. He is often seen clutching a serpent or a torque, two objects traditionally associated with Cernunnos (and completely absent from any Pan myths). The god's home is exclusively in the forest and he is often accompanied by a bow or sword and many wild animals (the latter drawing parallels to depictions of Cernunnos on the Gundestrup Cauldron). When shown with the legs of an animal, they are never those of a goat, but most often a stag's, with many artists also using Cernunnos's traditional sitting posture.

Like most people I did not grow up knowing anything about Cernunnos, and the deities I most dreamed about in my younger days were those of Greeks and the Norse. These were both pantheons with extensive mythologies, and have been a near constant presence in television, movies, comic-books, and "sophisticated" literature for my entire life. Cernunnos was completely unknown to me until I picked up my first book depicting Wiccan-Witchcraft in 1994.[1]

Cernunnos's placement in Conway's book was not an outlier in the early 1990's, instead it was representative of the steady progress Cernunnos had made into becoming the most recognized "horned god" in Modern Paganism. His rise to prominence can be traced through both purported academic works, and more popular books written especially for the modern Pagan and Witch communities. (I'm not suggesting that Cernunnos's modern popularity is dependent solely upon written texts, as a devotee of the god, I like to think that He played a role in this as well.)

If I were asked to name the one individual most responsible for Cernunnos's place in Modern Paganism I'd reply with Dr. Margaret Alice Murray (1863-1963). Murray was an Egyptologist by trade but became interested in the Witchcraft trials of the early modern period (1500-1800) during World War One while unable to travel outside of her native England. Her research during the war led her to write *The Witch-Cult in Western Europe* (1921) published by Oxford Press.

Murray's contention that Witchcraft was an organized religion in opposition to Christianity featuring a corrupted pagan deity transformed into the Devil, was never taken seriously by a majority of scholars, but Murray's work found a sympathetic ear in the general populace. By the 1960's her interpretation of the Witch trials had come to be considered "gospel" by many folks, a trend that continues into today. Murray's follow-up book in 1931, *The God of the Witches* (published by Faber and Faber, a popular press instead of an academic publisher) focused exclusively on her corrupted pagan deity and would mark the arrival of both Cernunnos and the "Horned God" as major figures in the soon to commence Pagan revival.

What makes *The God of the Witches* so profound is how powerfully Murray makes her case. No longer appearing as he did in *The Witch-Cult*, as the Devil dressed as a "man in black," Murray's deity was now the

Horned God (complete with the capital letters), and with a long and glorious history. Her Horned God was the most ancient of deities, stretching back to the 13,000-year-old figure known as "The Sorcerer" from Cave of the Trois-Frères in Southern France. From his cave origins, the Horned God then spreads throughout Europe, becoming known by a plethora of names including Pan, Herne, Robin Hood, and of course, Cernunnos.

Murray's mention of Cernunnos was not casual either. In *The God of the Witches* she refers to him as:

"A few rock carvings in Scandinavia show that the horned god was known there also in the Bronze age. It was only when Rome started on her career of conquest that any written record was made of the gods of western Europe, and those records prove that a horned deity, whom the Romans called Cernunnos, was one of the greatest gods, perhaps even the supreme deity, of Gaul."[2]

I find it unlikely that Cernunnos was the "supreme deity" in all of Gaul, but it's impossible not to get caught up in Murray's vision while reading this part of her book. Her Horned God was nature incarnate, and he came complete with rituals celebrating, life, death, and sex. When one finishes reading about Murray's Horned God it's something you find yourself wanting to go out and worship. (Never mind that Murray's Horned God is completely illogical, full of huge gaps in time, along with several uncomplimentary deities.)

Twenty years later the "horned god" would reappear in Gerald Gardner's (1884-1964) *Witchcraft Today*[3], as the god of a new and religious Witchcraft. But Gardner's mention of a horned god would not be Murray's only contribution to his text, she wrote the introduction to his book, sort of indirectly blessing the modern Witchcraft revival. Gardner, the English-speaking world's first public, self-identifying Witch, is one of the seminal architects of the Pagan Revival, and he was most likely influenced both directly and indirectly by Margaret Murray.

Gardner's 1959 follow-up book, *The Meaning of Witchcraft*, does not mention Cernunnos directly, but does include several mentions of the Horned God (now capitalized). One of those a description of the Horned One bears similarities to Cernunnos:

"Witches are constantly being accused of "worshipping the Devil". Now, when we use that word "Devil", what picture automatically forms itself in most people's minds? Is it not that of a strange-looking being who seems to be partly human and partly animal, having great horns on his head,

*and a body covered with hair, although his face is human? Have you ever
stopped to wonder why this picture should automatically come into your
mind in this way? There is not one single text in the Bible which describes
"the Devil" or "Satan" in this manner."*[4]

Gardner follows this description by linking his Horned God to Trois
Freres and the Sorcerer in France, basically following the guidebook given
by Murray.

Gardner's Horned God is linked to modern ideas about Cernunnos
in other ways. He writes of the Horned God as "the Lord of the Gates of
Death" and "the dealer of death."[5] But death would was not the only
function of the god; to Gardner he was also the "provider of food" and
when in a more poetic frame of mind Gardner writes that the Goddess
and Horned God of Witchcraft:

*". . . . came because man wanted magical rites for hunting; the prop-
er rites to procure increase in flocks and herds, to assure good fishing,
and to make women fruitful; then, later, rites for good farming, etc., and
whatever the clan needed, including help in time of war, to cure the sick,
and to hold and regulate the greater and lesser festivals, to conduct the
worship of the Goddess and the Horned God. They considered it good that
men should dance and be happy, and that this worship and initiation was
necessary for obtaining a favourable (sic) place in the After- World, and
a reincarnation into your own tribe again, among those whom you loved
and who loved you, and that you would remember, know, and love them
again."*[6]

A little over ten years after *The Meaning of Witchcraft*, the first "how
to" book on Modern Pagan Witchcraft was released by a major publisher. Until the publication of *Mastering Witchcraft: A Practical Guide for
Witches, Warlocks, and Covens* by Paul Huson in 1970 (GP Putnam &
Sons) the only way to obtain Witchcraft rituals was to either make them
up yourself or become an initiate in an established coven. Huson's work
made it easy to establish one's own personal Witchcraft practice, and not
surprisingly, Cernunnos featured prominently.

Early in the text Huson calls Cernunnos one of the "so-called Witch
deities"[7] he then later links Cernunnos to the imagery of Pan as part of
a greater Horned One:

"The goat is the age-old representation of lust and debauchery, and
Cernunnos himself, for such is his witch name, is frequently represented
as possessing the cloven hooves, horns, and erect phallus of his attribute.

His symbolism has much in common with that of the Greek god Pan . . . .

. . . . Whenever you wish to perform a spell whose object is to boggle someone's mind with lust, you should invoke holy Cernunnos . . ."[8]

At this point, at least in Witch literature, Pan and Cernunnos have for all intents and purposes become parts of the greater Horned One, with Cernunnos reigning as the "witch god."

Cernunnos would also feature in Huson's work as a god of vengeance. The god figures prominently in a work on poppet magick, which utilizes the power of Cernunnos to "vengefully stab the Dagyde (exorcised "needles of the art") into the part of the puppet designated for torment with the words 'so mote it be!'"[9] Later in the same chapter on "Vengeance and Attack" the power of Cernunnos is used to call up an electrical storm (but only on Tuesdays).[10]

Huson's work has been wildly influential over the last 50 years, and as the first "how to" book on Witchcraft ever published, his vision of Cernunnos has likely influenced thousands of people. Even today, it remains a best-seller on Witchcraft lists, and has found a second life as a guidebook for the emerging practice of "Traditional Witchcraft."

Huson's work is full of information, spells, and magickal formulas, but it's light on Witch ritual. In 1971 the first mostly complete book of Witch ritual was published by Llewellyn Publications. *Lady Sheba's Book of Shadows* (birth name Jessie Wicker Bell, 1920-2002) didn't belong to Lady Sheba at all, but was originally an oathbound Book of Shadows belonging to a Witch coven in England. Sheba's book is short on information but does contain eight sabbat rituals and the opening and closing frames of Wiccan-Witchcraft.

There Sheba lists the god and goddess of the Witches as "Arida and Kernunnos"[11] and repeats those names several times throughout her text. At the Spring Equinox Sheba's work calls Cernunnos the "Merciful Son of Cerridwen" and states that his "name is Highest of all."[12] The most common chant in the book features the lines "EKO EKO ARIDA, EKO EKO KERNUNNOS"[13] reinforcing the link between what I suppose is meant to be "Aradia" and Cernunnos.

Sheba's work removes Cernunnos from his place as the god of vengeance (as seen in Huson) and returns him firmly to the realm of death. Her "Hallowmass Sabbat" (Samhain is linked to the Autumn Equinox in the work) features the Horned God Cernunnos (or Kernunnos) as "Dread Lord of Shadows, God of Life and Bringer of Death."[14] This attribute first hinted at by Gardner, would become a familiar one amongst followers of the god.

Why Sheba uses the "K" spelling of Cernunnos is worth speculating on. It's possible that the god's name was spelled this way in the original Book of Shadows she received. Or perhaps she was attempting to recreate a name had simply heard previously and not seen written down. Sheba's curious spelling would not become all that common, but it does show up from time to time in Witch books written in the 1970's.

Links to Cernunnos and Pan would continue during the 1970's, with Doreen Valiente (1922-1999) calling him "the Celtic horned god, similar to Pan" in 1978's *Witchcraft for Tomorrow*.[15] In that same work she used a corrupted version of his name in her "Word of Power" again in combination with Aradia. "IA IA ARADIA! IO EVOHE KERNUNNO!"[16]

The most important Witch works of the 1980's to feature Cernunnos were *Eight Sabbats for Witches* (1981) and *The Witches' Way* (originally published by Robert Hale in England, and Phoenix Publishing in the United States, both books feature in the combined *A Witches' Bible* in 1996) by Janet and Stewart Farrar. There not only is Cernunnos spelled properly, but he is again used as the principal male Witch deity, though not surprisingly he is again linked to Pan. (Written along with Doreen Valiente, *Eight Sabbats for Witches* is a previously unpublished Book of Shadows, allegedly influenced by Gardner's covens.)

At the end of an invocation to Cernunnos the Farrars call Cernunnos the "Shepherd of Goats."[17] Other than this aside, Cernunnos generally fills the role first spelled out by Murray and Gardner: that of a deity of both life and death. In the work of the Farrars he also shows up again in the "Eko Eko" chants first published by Sheba, and his name is invoked at the start of every ritual. (The Farrars use him in their "opening frame" which is designed to begin every sabbat rite.)

Due to his appearances in books by the Farrars, Sheba, Huson, and others, by the 1990's the image of Cernunnos had become the default "Horned God." Cernunnos's identification as "Celtic" (and not limited to his native Gaul) most likely also helped with the popularity of his image. In 1993's *To Ride a Silver Broomstick* (Llewellyn Publications) Silver Ravenwolf calls Cernunnos "Celtic; Horned God and consort of the Lady. Also Kernunnos."[18] Due to the prominence of Wiccan-Witchcraft in the 1990s and the rise of interest in "Celtic" music and mythology images and veneration of Cernunnos spread from Witch culture into the greater Pagan world, and have generally stayed there.

Today it's impossible to visit a metaphysical store without seeing a modern interpretation of Cernunnos on a resin statue or plaque. Images inspired by him adorn necklaces and t-shirts from both independent Pagan artisans and mass marketers of consumer goods. Due to the god's popularity in the greater Pagan world, it's likely that his reach and power extend much further now than they ever did during his original heyday in ancient Gaul.

hail Cernunnos.

[1] That book was *Celtic Magic* by DJ Conway, first published by Llewellyn in 1990. Cernunnos is listed as "The Horned God" on page 106.

[2] My edition of *God of the Witches* was published in 2005 by NuVision Publications. This quote appears there on page 21. The edition I have is identical to Murray's 1931 edition.

[3] Gardner's book has a few things in it we would identify today with Wiccan-Witchcraft, and a lot of other stuff that doesn't really resonate. In the book he makes only one reference to a horned god of Witches, and doesn't capitalize it.

[4] Gerald Gardner writing in *The Meaning of Witchcraft*, first published in 1959 by Rider & Co. I'm using the Magickal Childe edition from 1991. This quote appears on page 20 of that edition

[5] Ibid, page 45.

[6] Ibid, page 25.

[7] Huson Paul, *Mastering Witchcraft*, Perigree/Berkely books, 1970, page 32. I'm quoting from the Perigree Books edition from 1980.

[8] Ibid, pages 120-121

[9] Ibid page 196,

[10] Ibid page 201

[11] Bell, Jessie Wicker, *The Grimoire of Lady Sheba*, Llewellyn Publications, originally published in 1972, I'm using the 2001 hardback edition, page 119. The Grimoire was released a year after Lady Sheba's Book of Shadows, and includes the original Book of Shadows and additional material.

[12] Ibid, page 205.

[13] Ibid, page 227, and other places.

[14] Ibid, page 237

[15] Valiente, Doreen, *Witchcraft for Tomorrow*, Robert Hale Ltd., 1978.

[16] Ibid, page 163. Here she also includes the names Diana and Pan.

[17] Farrar, Janet & Stewart, *The Witches' Bible*, Phoenix Publishing, 1996, originally from *Eight Sabbats for Witches*.

[18] Ravenwolf, Silver, *To Ride a Silver Broomstick*, Llewellyn Publications, 1993, page 53.

SER-nun-nos or Ser-NUN-nos?
KER-nun-nos or Ker-NUN-nos?
Stephen Posch

The Old Gaulish antlered god Cernunnos is hot these days. (Ask me, He's always been hot.) So how do you pronounce His Name?

SER-nun-nos or Ser-NUN-nos? KER-nun-nos or Ker-NUN-nos?

Well, how you pronounce your god's name is up to you and certainly none of my business. But if you'd like to know the historical pronunciation – how, for instance, whoever carved the famous Paris Cernunnos relief would have said it – there historical linguistics can help you.

Historically speaking, we can rule out the first two pronunciations immediately. In Gaulish, C was always "hard" (i.e. pronounced as K).

So, KER-nun-nos or Ker-NUN-nos? One hears both pronunciations these days. (I've never heard anyone attempt ker-nun-NOS, praise His Horns.)

Well, we can't say with absolute certainty that it's one or the other, since Gaulish has been a dead language for considerably more than a millennium. According to Dutch linguist Peter Schrijver, however, available evidence indicates that, as a rule, the Gaulish language favored stress on the penultimate (next-to-the-last) syllable.

So, if by some chance you should happen to find yourself transported back through time to Roman era *Lutetia* (Paris) and ask passers-by in the street after ker-NUN-nos, chances are that they'll understand you well enough to be able to point you to His nearest temple.

Which, under the circumstances, might not be a bad place to start.

Source: Peter Schrijver (1995), *Studies in British Historical Phonology*. Amsterdam: Rodopi

herne and Cernunnos
Jason Mankey

When I embraced Witchcraft and Paganism in the 1990s most books that included information on male deities equated the English Herne with Cernunnos. In Janet and Stewart Farrar's *The Witch's God* (1989) Cernunnos and Herne share a chapter and are basically written about as if they were the same god. Not surprisingly writers such as the Farrars were drawing from the works of Margaret Murray, who also conflated Herne with Cernunnos (and the Greek Pan, but that's another story). The mingling of the two deities has continued into the present, with many images of Herne looking similar to popular depictions of Cernunnos.

It must be said that Cernunnos and Herne do sort of sound alike. Dropping the last two syllables from Cernunnos (but leaving in the "n" sound) leaves us with "cern" which rhymes with Herne, a conflation which has been used to explain the idea that Herne is the English version of the Gallic Cernunnos. But Herne and Cernunnos are very different deities and have nothing in common other than superficial similarities. Cernunnos is a deity that can be found on altars and steles, Herne is a figure that comes to us from (likely) folktales and literature.

The first mention of Herne occurs in William Shakespeare's 1597 play *The Merry Wives of Windsor*. In that play Herne shares more in common with ghosts than he does Celtic deities:

"There is an old tale that goes Herne the Hunter
Sometimes a keeper in Windsor Forest,
Doth all the winter-time, at still midnight,
Walk round about an oak, with great ragg'd horns;
And there he blasts the tree, and takes the cattle,
And makes milche-kine yield blood, and shakes a chain
In a most hideous and dreadful manner.
You have heard of such a spirit, and well you know
The superstitious idle-headed old
Receiv'd and did deliver to our age,
This tale of Herne the Hunter for a truth.

Other than the great "ragg'd horns" Herne and Cernunnos share no physical similarities. Cernunnos did not carry a chain, and it's unlikely that a torc would have been magically turned into a chain 1400 years after the heyday of our favorite Gallic deity. The activities of Herne in Shake-speare's play are also problematic, it's hard to imagine Cernunnos blasting trees, taking cattle, and appearing in a "most hideous and dreadful man-ner." What we know about Cernunnos in no way matches Shakespeare's ghostly depiction of Herne.

Given the late date of *Merry Wives* it's also possible that Shakespeare made up Herne specifically for his play. While I find this unlikely, *The Merry Wives of Windsor* contains several bits of folklore from the Wind-sor are that were documented before Shakespeare's play was performed and published, it has to at least be considered. Only after Shakespeare's publication of *Merry Wives* do mentions of Herne living in Windsor For-est appear with regularity.

One of the most interesting mentions of Herne involves a tree in the great Windsor Forest that was known as "Herne's Oak." Though cut down in 1796, the tree was so well known that it sometimes made appearances in the area's local newspaper beginning in 1742. (In these early mentions of Herne's Oak the tree is called "Sir John Falstaff's Oak," named after another figure from Shakespeare's play.[1]) Drawings of the tree exist into the present day as do a few alleged pieces of wood from it. A great tree is essential to most versions of the Herne story, being the spot where Herne chose to end his own life (or was executed) via hanging.

The figure of Herne hanging from a great oak tree is one of the most consistent elements among the variable stories about Herne. Some ver-sions of his tale involve him being restored to life after being gored by a stag in service to his king as a keeper of the forest, the stag's horns added to the top of his head during the process. Sadly for Herne though, in these versions of the story he is returned to the world of the living without his woodland skills due to the jealousy of his fellow keepers, and chooses to end his own life via hanging than living as a shell of himself. After his suicide, Herne returns to the living as a ghost to seek vengeance.

Vengeance is a common theme in the stories of Herne. Instead of end-ing his own life, he is executed (via hanging) for poaching in the Windsor Forest. A more shocking version of the story has Herne returning to the world of the living to avenge his daughter who was defiled by the King. In all of these stories Herne is not a figure to be trifled with, or even sought out. His appearance is ghostly and his countenance grim. Upon his return from the dead Herne was often thought to hunt through the woods with a spectral hunting party, invoking shades of the Wild Hunt.

Herne's hanging has parallels with another Pagan god, and if Herne is truly related to an ancient pagan deity it's more like to be Odin or Woden than the Gallic Cernunnos. The two deities share being hung upon a tree, and both figures have been linked to spectral hunting parties. The Vikings settled in England during the Ninth and Tenth Centuries, which means the figure known as Herne would have spent less time "underground" before being written about than if he were related to Cernunnos.

Curiously we could also have Herne's name completely wrong. A pirate edition of *The Merry Wives of Windsor* published in 1602 includes a few additional lines about Herne, here spelled "Horne:"

> Oft have you heard since Horne the hunted dyed,
> That women to affright their little children,
> Ses that he walkes in shape of a great stagge.[2]

During the reign of King Henry VIII in the first half of the 16th century a parchment currently in the British Museum tells of a hunter named Rycharde Horne who was executed for poaching in the Windsor Forest. Could Rycharde Horne be Herne? Or perhaps Horne's story was added to another existing ghost story from the area? It's also worth noting that Odin survived in folktales long after the Scandinavian countries converted to Christianity. Stories of Odin, Rycharde Horne, and an existing ghost legend could have all converged to create tales of the figure we now call Herne.

It seems likely that Herne and Cernunnos will continue to be associated to some degree as the conflation between the two deities still shows up in books and blogs. It is my hope though, that the differences between the two figures will eventually encourage people to treat them as separate deities.

[1] Fitch, Eric, L., *In Search of Herne the Hunter*, Capall Bann Publishing, 1994, pages 23-4
[2] Fitch, page 11

Cernunnos Denton
John Beckett

Polytheism is likely humanity's default religious position: it is intuitive that there are many Gods. The Sun God and the Moon Goddess are not the same person. The Rain Goddess and the God of the Desert are not the same person. I became convinced of this in 2004 when I spent nine nights in meditation with the deities of the Egyptian Ennead. It was clear that Isis and Osiris were different persons, and both were different from Shu and Tefnut and the other deities of Heliopolis.

Polytheism is so intuitive that monotheists have to wage a never-ending war against the many Gods. If they don't, their followers will slide from casually mentioning "the Weather Gods" and "the Gods of Baseball" to interacting with these Gods and then to worshipping Them – and many Others.

What is not so intuitive but was clearly understood to be true in ancient times is the multiplicity of individual deities. Egyptian religion was not fixed for 4000 years: worship, myths, and even the names of the Gods changed over the centuries. In ancient Greece, Zeus Olympios was understood and worshipped differently from Zeus Chthonios and Zeus Aetnaeus. Athena Parthenos, Athena Nike, and Athena Polias were and are understood differently, but all are Athena.

Do these changes from place to place and time to time mean there are multiple individual deities with the same name? Or perhaps they're different in the way that John Beckett who lived in Tennessee at age 30 is different from John Beckett who lived in Texas at age 50? Perhaps the Gods are able to transcend time in ways that humans cannot and so all versions exist at all times? I don't know – the multiplicity of the Gods is a mystery I struggle to understand.

But I am increasingly certain that Cernunnos as we understand, experience, and worship Him here in Denton, Texas is a distinct instance of His multiplicity, and at the very least Cernunnos Denton is a proper epithet for Cernunnos.

Cernunnos Comes To Denton

In 2005 a good friend went to England for a visit. I had never been – I gave her a $20 and asked her to bring me a t-shirt. Instead, she brought back a medallion of "the Horned God." We did a little research and learned that the image on the medallion is from the Gundestrup Cauldron, a 2000 year old silver bowl covered with scenes from Celtic mythology, and that the God depicted is likely Cernunnos.

I say "likely" because we can't be sure, but as Jason Mankey points out in his opening essay, historical evidence points in that direction, and contemporary UPG (unverified personal gnosis) around it is so strong it should be called SPG (shared personal gnosis).

I began wearing the medallion in ritual and in meditation. And then one evening in 2006 a small group of Denton Pagans met in this same friend's back yard to perform a Drawing Down ritual. Only instead of drawing down into the High Priestess (as in Wiccan practice) the vessel was me. And instead of invoking The Goddess, we called to Cernunnos.

And he showed up.

The notes in my private journal (written the next morning) are rather vague. But though I cannot adequately put it into words, it was one of the most powerful and most real experiences of my life. A portion of Him merged with me. Only a portion – any more and I would have exploded, spiritually if not physically, though quite possibly that too. I got a taste of His power and His wisdom and His divinity and it was amazing.

My work with Cernunnos would get deeper.

The Cernunnos Ritual

I honored and communed with Cernunnos regularly over the following years. In 2013 He made it very clear that it was time for us to hold a public ritual for Him. For our first Cernunnos Ritual, we wanted to appeal to as many people as possible. Here's an excerpt from the introduction to that ritual:

Different ideas about the Gods make for interesting conversation, but tonight they're not important. Tonight what's important is that you experience Cernunnos, and if you are so moved, that you respond to Him. If you find yourself starting to wander into the realm of analysis, I encourage you to acknowledge the impulse, let it go, and give yourself permission to pick it up again after the ritual is over.

Experience now, analyze later.

We began with a procession. We made offerings to Cernunnos. We sang for Him. I told the story of my encounters with Him. We had a short call and response emphasizing our place as part of Nature, and His place as Lord of the Animals and Lord of the Hunt.

Then the drumming started and we began chanting His name. At that point the ritual script stopped. Now, I'm not comfortable with unscripted rituals. I like order and predictability. But I serve a God who is wild and free, and He only tolerates my obsessive orderliness so much.

His presence – which had been mild but undeniable since we started setting up – became overwhelming. Someone shouted. Someone got up and began to dance. Then another got up, and another, and another. Before long we had a whole line of people dancing, spinning, and chanting around the altar.

Cernunnos! Cernunnos! Cernunnos!

I don't know how long it went on. It was all I could do to hold on to my responsibilities as ritual leader and not get quite literally carried away with His presence. When the energy began to wane, I moved to the front of the altar and said a prayer of thanksgiving for the gathering and a prayer of hope for what would be taken away from the ritual.

Afterwards, He seemed pleased. But far from satisfied.

The Travels of Cernunnos Denton

We did the ritual again. Cynthia Talbot, my fellow priest and Denton Pagan, went with me to the 2013 OBOD East Coast Gathering, where we presented the Cernunnos Ritual again. Rather than a Unitarian Universalist meeting house, this ritual took place in a circle deep in the woods. Our procession was led by torchlight, and we had eight professional and near-professional drummers calling us in. As we were walking up the path I thought "this must be very close to what my ancient ancestors did."

This gathering was larger, and other than Cynthia and I, the participants were completely different. But we introduced Cernunnos as we understood and experienced him – we took the Denton tradition to Pennsylvania.

The response was much the same.

We presented the Cernunnos Ritual a third time in 2013, at the Dallas – Fort Worth Pagan Pride Day. This was at White Rock Lake Park, the largest and most popular public park in the city of Dallas. The openness of that ritual – both in terms of its participants and in terms of its physical location – created some challenges, but He was still there, and I still occasionally hear people talking about the ritual.

In 2017 we presented a revised version of the Cernunnos Ritual at Beltane that addressed the political fears people were feeling at the time. And in August of that year, Jason Mankey, Kirk Thomas, and I led the ritual at the Beyond the Gates retreat at Trout Lake Abbey, Washington. Gwion Raven was our drummer.

Cernunnos as we first experienced Him in Denton in 2005 has now travelled from Texas to both coasts of the United States, and from there around the country and around the world.

At first I thought all that was travelling was our tradition – our way of honoring Cernunnos. But that changed at Beltane 2017.

A Painting of Cernunnos Denton

Morgan Milburn created a painting of Cernunnos for an art class. When the class was done she gave the painting to me, at our Beltane ritual honoring Him. At first I called it "Portrait of a Priesthood" since so much of it seemed so personal to me. But the more I thought about it – and the more I came down from the emotional high of receiving this beautiful gift – the more I realized it's not about me. It's about Him.

This isn't another derivative of the Gundestrup Cauldron, or of the Pillar of the Boatmen (which is how we know the name Cernunnos). This is an original work of art that depicts the emergence of Cernunnos in Denton.

After two years of contemplation – and of sleeping under this picture most every night (it hangs in my bedroom) – I am convinced it is the first depiction of Cernunnos Denton. And I'm also convinced it will not be the last.

What is Cernunnos Denton? Who is Cernunnos Denton?

Is Cernunnos Denton simply a convenient way of saying "Cernunnos, as He's understood and experienced by Pagans in Denton, Texas"? Or is Cernunnos Denton a distinct individual deity who has come into existence of His own will in order to relate to us living here and now, and those like us? I do not know.

What I do know is that He is the Lord of the Animals and the Lord of the Hunt. He is a God of the Wild in a society where wild places are increasingly hard to find. He is a protector and a nurturer in an environment of exploitation.

And He is calling people to work with Him and for Him to promote His values and virtues, to respect the Earth and all Her creatures, to end human-caused extinctions, to remember that for all the benefits of civilization we are still animals who need to at least occasionally experience the wild.

And sometimes, He calls us to dance around a fire, chanting His name.

Blessed be Cernunnos.

Blessed be Cernunnos Denton.

Cernunnos Denton
Morgan Milburn

Cernunnos as a Lost Dionysian Twin: Recent Celticist Scholarship and its Implications for Practitioners

M. X. Petrovich, Ph.D.
University of Oxford, UK

Abstract:

This essay takes the recent monograph, Cernunnos, *le dioscure sauvage: Recherches comparatives sur la divinité dionysiaque des Celtes* (Paris, 2010) by two renowned scholars of Celtic art history and literatures, Daniel Gricourt and Dominique Hollard, as its point of departure, proceeding to discuss the developing understanding of Cernunnos away from the standard interpretation as a barely documented Gaulish deity toward a more complex analysis of his layered connection to medieval Celtic lore. In addition to a critical review of the monograph, the essay also addresses the dynamics through which such scholarly works might be understood or disseminated in Neopagan communities, and the ways in which popular perceptions of Cernunnos resemble those of Celticist scholarship or differ from them. Finally, a few suggestions on Neopagan practice are made.

Main text

1.   The Old Cernunnos: Wicca and Celtic Mystique

The disjunction between scholarly and non-academic audiences on the subject of Cernunnos has grown in recent decades, as old certitudes are being called into question and novel methods are devised to work with familiar sources, be they of visual or textual nature.[1] To this intellectual climate might be added the current cultural and social crisis across the Atlantic world, which has led to renewed engagement with what might be termed "the deep roots of Europe" and which has not always produced sound or savoury arguments.[2] Books with Cernunnos on the cover exert a pull of intense masculine mystery, regardless of their content; indeed, the publisher, the author and the reader alike might not be able or willing to disentangle Cernunnos from Pan, Herne or the more generic Wiccan Horned God, as long as he inspires...and sells.[3]

As in many other fields, academic specialists are not precisely eager to interact with polytheist or pagan circles (cue in the cruel moniker for many non-professional Egypt enthusiasts and Kemeticists used among scholars, "pyramidiots").[4] Professional Celticists are more polite in their discomfort with popular discourses, which usually include echoes of Margaret Murray's thesis on the God of the Witches and Robert Graves's analysis of the "tree alphabet" on the English side, as well as the lyrical reimaginings of Druids by the prolific Jean Markale (born as Jean Bertrand) on the French side: for all their impact upon popular imagination, scholars tend to ignore them, which is all the easier since Graves did not read Welsh or medieval Irish, and Markale similarly did not work directly with Breton or Welsh.[5]

The two approaches seem to be divided by an insurmountable abyss, as even those audiences who do seek to be informed about most recent developments in scholarship are blocked by shrinking and fragmented library resources.[6] The internet has been a double-edged sword, sprouting highly questionable theories and memes, but also opening up resources to people coming from all socio-economic classes to an unprecedented extent. The availability of hitherto obscure dictionaries, grammars and nineteenth-century editions of primary sources has created a new kind of what I term here the "lay scholar" (analogous to lay clergy), typified by well-known pagans such as Morgan Daimler.[7] Curiously, one of the side effects has been a subterranean return to German-speaking Celticists of yore such as Rudolf Thurneysen, Kuno Meyer and Julius Pokorný.[8]

Still, with a handful of exceptions, most Neopagans who are interested in Celtic gods tend to focus on visual evidence rather than on linguistics[9]; it is a testimony to the difficulty of Old and Middle Irish (and the relative scarcity of its lexicographic tools) that Old Norse and Middle Egyptian sources are much more often cited in those circles; however, there has been a recent linguistically-informed movement to reconstruct the Gaulish language and create a devotional literature, lauded by professional Celticists.[10]

While the Cernunnos of the Gundestrup cauldron has become an iconic and instantly recognizable image even for those who know very little about Celtic history, other Celtic deities have also gained in popularity in the last two decades. Notable among them is the ascendance of the Mórrígan (I use this spelling with the meaning of "Great Queen" consciously, pace Stokes), on whom several books were authored in the last few years with the aim of merging Celticist scholarship (usually mediated through nineteenth-century translations into English or occasionally German) with a ritual practice.[11] Indeed, the cultural phenomenon of the "Call of the Mórrígan" deserves a separate article.[12] Even if we should be so churlish as to suggest that the enthusiasm for Cernunnos or the Mórrígan are mere trends or fashions, that phenomenon surely still deserves to be studied in terms of its cultural and social importance, and what the admiration for, say, the Tuatha Dé Danann, says about contemporary English-speaking societies.

This article, written by a professional historian with a training in historical linguistics and comparative literature (albeit not a Celticist), seeks to bridge the gap between two kinds of knowledge, the one popular and adventurously speculative, the other recondite and cautiously scholarly, by summarizing and discussing a recent French monograph on Cernunnos and indicating some intellectual and theological implications of its arguments.[13]

2. A New Cernunnos? Recent Findings and Analysis

The voluminous study Cernunnos, *le dioscure sauvage: Recherches comparatives sur la divinité dionysiaque des Celtes* (Paris, 2010) by Daniel Gricourt and Dominique Hollard announces some of its findings in its title: *Cernunnos, the Wild Twin: Comparative Studies on the Dionysian Deity of the Celts*.[14] Both authors are professional numismatists and specialists in the iconography of the Celto-Roman period working at the Bibliothèque nationale in Paris. Notably, their expertise includes textual sources relevant to Celts, including epigraphy in Gaulish, as well as facility with more extensive literary corpora in Latin, Greek, Welsh and Irish Gaelic. As part of the established scholarly tradition, they also address Indo-European connections in Middle Persian and Ossetic as well as Vedic and post-Vedic Sanskrit materials. Crucially, the framework is thoroughly comparativist; more will be said on that in the conclusion.[15] In the following and the footnotes, the monograph will be abbreviated as CDS.

A significant virtue of their study resides in its extensive bibliography which cannot be ignored by anyone with a serious interest in Cernunnos. CDS inserts itself immediately into the most recent academic debates on Cernunnos, addressing the works by Claude Sterckx, of the Université libre of Brussels, Bernard Sergent, of the renowned CNRS (*Centre national de la recherche scientifique*) in Paris and Patrice Lajoye, of the Université de Caen in Normandy.

CDS opens with a reaction to the following elegant statement by Patrice Lajoye to which most might initially subscribe: "Cernunnos is a phenomenon. Although he belongs to an Indo-European pantheon, he is one of a kind (*unique dans son genre*) by his posture, by his physical attributes, and above all by the difficulty he poses to scholarly research because of the lack of comparative points of reference (*repère*)."[16] The authors of CDS respectfully disagree with this assessment, claiming instead that the evidence suggests that the much-lamented lack of textual sources on Cernunnos is merely apparent rather than substantial and that perhaps it is possible to fill in the blanks.

Turning briefly to the other scholars: within the framework of a formidable three-volume study, Sterckx has suggested that Cernunnos should be identified as one of the attributes of the Jupiterian God Taranis. [17] In his equally renowned work, published as a series of studies called *Celto-Hellenica*, the exceedingly prolific Sergent has explored the processes by which homologous deities of the Roman Celtic world emerged, with relatively unsurprising analogies in terms of function such as Poseidon and Manannán, Hephaistos and Goibniu. More intriguingly, within his framework, Zeus is equated with Taranis, Apollo with Lugus, Hermes with Óengus and, perhaps most unexpectedly, Athena with Badb and the Mórrígan.[18] Sergent is significant here because he also wrote the introduction to CDS, expressing both admiration and discomfort with its findings.[19]

To vastly oversimplify a complex and encyclopaedic argument, CDS revolves around several mythopoetic themes. One of them is Cernunnos as a Dionysian twin and sexual rival to an Apollonic Lugus; another, a hitherto ignored aquatic aspect to Cernunnos; yet another, the cyclical appearance of Cernunnos as either a young boy or a mature virile man and stag. Ancillary discussions include lengthy digressions on the semiotics of Artemis as a deer-hunter and on the Mother Goddess who rejects some of her children; the authors also address numerous medieval reinterpretations of those themes, particularly within the Old and Middle Irish, Welsh and French literary traditions.

A core aspect upon which the argument of CDS rests is the potential common genealogy between Cernunnos and his Indo-European cognates, antedating the Roman conquest of Gaul, and called by them a "theological inheritance" in the shape of a Celtic-Greek-Indic triangle. [20] Parallels between Dionysos and Śiva are well-known, as they were first suggested by the vastly gifted, but also callous and opportunistic French musicologist and Sanskritist Alain Daniélou in his 1979 book which gained much additional currency by virtue of its translation into English.[21] Daniélou and Joseph Campbell (!) were also among the first to suggest an analogy between Cernunnos and Śiva, further briefly investigated in an article by Glenys Goetinck in 1995.[22] The third side of Indo-Greek-Celtic triangle, as suggested by the authors of CDS, consists in investigating some striking similarities between Dionysos and Cernunnos from a Celtic perspective, particularly their shared iconographies.[23]

Another component which will be familiar to at least some American audiences is the equation of Cernunnos with the god whose antlers fall off and regrow seasonally, as the chthonic aspects of the divine masculine dominate the cold half of the year, starting with Samhain and ending with Bealtaine. Scholarly reference is here to the deceased Jean-Jacques Hatt, in articles from the 1960s and his subsequent study on Gaulish myths and Gods.[24] The summer counterpart of the telluric Cernunnos is, of course, the avian Lugus and his "cognates", the Irish Lugh mac Ethnenn and the Welsh Lleu Llaw Gyffes.[25]

CDS takes these relatively uncontroversial hypotheses as their points of departure to suggest other pieces of the puzzle. Rather than being equated with Taranis/Jupiter as Sterckx would have it, in the authors' interpretation, Cernunnos is to be seen firmly as the Celtic equivalent to Dionysos, (who, ancient aspersions of a barbarian Thracian or Phrygian origin to the contrary, is a solidly Greek god attested even in the Mycenaean period). The seasonal alteration of Apollo and Dionysos at the shrine of Delphi indicates that their Celtic equivalents, the gods of summer and winter, are unequivocally Lugus and the Cernunnos, who engage in a seasonal battle for the favour of a somewhat generic figure of the Goddess, perhaps to be equated with the fertile Earth.

The authors delve deeper into this particular aspect, elucidating a paradox. The horns/antlers of Cernunnos which signal his virility are thus also an indication of his seasonal transformation into a cuckold.[26] Since this is an inevitable and even eternal occurrence, it is possible that at least in the pre-Christian period no particular shame or humiliation was attached to his temporary defeat. Indeed, Lugus suffers the same fate during the darker part of the year and on a few depictions he even sports a rudimentary head of antlers. CDS helpfully delves into the biology of the deer mating cycle, pointing out that the timing of the loss and acquisition of antlers closely mirror the division of the Celtic ritual year.[27]

The theme of adultery displayed great tenacity through the centuries, as it perpetuated itself in Middle Welsh and the Irish sagas, subsequently permeating medieval courtly literature, mostly through the medium of Old French. An immediate equivalent can obviously be found in the *Fourth Branch of the Mabinogi*, the tale of Math fab Mathonwy, which details the betrayal of Lleu Llaw Gyffes by his wife Blodeuwedd. The equivalent to Cernunnos in this context would be her lover Gronw Pebr, known as a hunter of deer. Other, more obscure, parallels are brought up by the authors of CDS, perhaps the most plausible of which is the rivalry of the Lughian Fionn mac Cumhaill and the Cernunnian Dearg Corra (the "Red Horn"). Other examples, such as the unavoidable Tristan, King March and Yseult, are also given.[28]

So far, so good, whether in respectable Celticist or Wiccan circles, one might say. But an additional insight is somewhat astonishing and potentially far-reaching. The column of Nautae Parisiaci, with one of the rare epigraphic attestations of Cernunnos, depicts the divine twins (Διόσκουροι), the "celestial" Pollux and the "infernal" Castor along with their Gaulish equivalents Smertrios and Cernunnos.[29] Rather than the traditional association with Ares/Mars, CDS suggests that Smertios, the foresighted one, is a representation (*epiclèse*) of Lugus, which leads to the conclusion that Lugus and the Cernunnos are not only rivals, but also twins.[30] By extension, *any twins* of Lugh/Lleu from Irish and Welsh sources would actually refer to aspects of youthful Cernunnos under a different name, rejected by his mother, in this instance Arianrhod.

Such conclusions might seem tenuous at first glance, but they do rest upon solid and subtle reasoning. The depiction of Castor as a double of Cernunnos on the Nautae Parisiaci column draws attention to the meaning of his name in French and Latin, "beaver", an animal with a clearly aquatic aspect. Most readers would see this detail as minor and even incongruous, but in fact it demonstrates a deep understanding of Cernunnos as a deity who straddles the chthonic and the aquatic, as the amphibious beaver does. The suggestion becomes even more plausible once the authors explain that the deer is actually also described as a semi-aquatic animal in traditional lore, able to cross rivers by swimming. Finally, a river by his name is attested in today's Lorraine region (Sânon, described as *fluvius Cernuni* in 699), and British depictions of Cernunnos show him with an eel-like lower extremity. The authors stress that this does not mean that Cernunnos is an aquatic deity, but rather than he has an recurring aquatic component, similar to Dionysos.[31]

The aquatic hypothesis finally explains the depiction of a child figure wearing the same "bodysuit" (*justaucorps*) as Cernunnos and riding a dolphin on the very same panel of the Gundestrup Cauldron: the child is Cernunnos himself, simultaneously young and old (hence, ageless). From there, the authors draw another insightful analogy to Merlin/Myrddin Wyllt/Lailoken, described in medieval Latin sources as a semi-demented *homo silvaticus*, one who is a boy and an old man simultaneously (*puer et senex*), and who suffers multiple painful deaths only to be reborn.[32] Echoes of Dionysos and his multiple deaths and rebirths, as recounted most famously by Nonnos of Panopolis in his Dionysiaca (Διονυσιακά), do resonate strongly here.[33]

Once the reader accepts the possibility that the child figure on the Gundestrup Cauldron is Cernunnos himself, an entire world of connections to epigones and homologues opens up, starting with the *Mabinogi* and the seemingly marginal figure of Dylan ail Ton ("of the waves"), the brother of Lleu who at the first glance perishes shortly after birth by falling into water and then turning into a dolphin or a seal, thus passing through death in order to achieve rebirth in an animal form. CDS also speculates that such connections shed light on the real importance of Maponos alias Mabon ap Modron, who was not only an abandoned child, but also a renowned hunter of the wild boar Twrch Trwyth through his association with the dog Drudwyn, both of which are animals associated with Cernunnos.[34]

The closing chapter of CDS emphasizes characteristics of Cernunnos with which most readers, scholarly or speculative, would readily agree: Having experienced a violent series of deaths since his earliest childhood, he is a shamanic figure who dies and returns to life in several elements. [35] As a child, he appears to be amphibious and akin to seals and dolphins. As an adult, he matures into a stag. His cervid presence in wild nature evokes a consistent association with fertility and abundance, complemented by his chthonic self which is represented by the ram-headed snake and which allows him to rule over underground treasures as well.

The authors conclude that the multiple lineages of Cernunnos confirm the assertion made by Bernard Robreau that Celtic shamanism contains at least two vital strands, one stemming from nomadic Iranian speakers such as the Scythians who migrated into Europe from the

Pontic-Caspian steppe, while the other, much older one, predates the arrival of any Indo-Europeans by thousands of years.[36] Accordingly, the pre-Celtic aspect of Cernunnos is indeed one the oldest attested deities, as he can be traced to Neolithic and perhaps even Palaeolithic times.[37]

Which conclusions can we draw from this cursory journey through this seminal work?

First of all, a purely technical note. There is a serious flaw relevant to the scholarly apparatus, as no index of any kind is included, and the reader must constantly refer to the table of contents instead. Such decisions are usually made by the publisher rather than the authors, but this certainly needs to be rectified in any future editions.

Since the authors are brave enough to cite popular literature authored by Joseph Campbell, one also wonders to what extent they allowed for side glances at Neopagan works of the more elaborate and scholarly kind, for instance the very informed book by Alexei Kondratiev, who taught Irish and other Celtic languages at the Irish Arts Center in New York city until his passing in 2010. Kondratiev's best-known work, *The Apple Branch*, suggests ritual practices which include historically attested invocations in Irish, Welsh and Breton, and in its introduction, it includes an extensive informed discussion about the history of Celtic peoples. It is uncertain whether the authors of CDS indeed used Kondratiev's book, although many themes do resonate across their own monograph. Either way, it is remarkable that *The Apple Branch*, in spite of its flaws and idealizations of a primordial "Celtic" identity, is much more on the scholarly side than on that of the "fluffy" New Age works with which it might be superficially compared.[38]

Back to CDS: Its readers might well be incredulous about some aspects of the work. Even if CDS occasionally seems to "connect everything with everything" in its sheer exuberance, the alternative, at least within the scholarship, is to retain a mysterious Cernunnos who is essentially a scant set of images devoid of context. Such minimalist and cautious approaches have their validity within academic discourse, but in the process of avoiding implausible flights of fancy, they face a different risk, namely, becoming trapped in a self-imposed aridity which ignores all possibilities of cross-connections for the sake of safety.[39]

While a suggested Dionysian twin definition of Cernunnos can be easily accepted, this reviewer admits to initial difficulties assimilating the aquatic component of the argument, along with its extended implication of other names of young Cernunnos in Welsh lore. But many details provided by the authors are ultimately convincing in their entirety. Ultimately, the reviewer was convinced by two details; first, the dolphin connection between Cernunnos and Dionysos, and second, the knowledge that the chthonic and the aquatic are connected, as they are both traditional environments of the underworld and the spirits.

Indeed, it seems that the authors intend to supplement this study with a further one on Cernunnos as a psychopomp, which is something to look forward to. Perhaps the Myrddin Wyllt hypothesis can be extended there, along with the unaddressed question of parallels between the chthonic Cernunnos and Gwyn ap Nudd and his rule over Annwn. The tension between Cernunnos as a protector of the animal world (would that even include plants?) and his role as a master over the riches of the underworld who allows mining of stones is also unresolved.

3.   Working with a God – Some Neopagan Implications

As for the theme of adultery, far beyond being a prurient and amusing tale similar to that of Ares and Hephaistos vying for Aphrodite, the *mythème*, as the authors call it, seems to belong among the deepest *mysteries* of the pre-Roman Celtic beliefs, illustrating a perennial cycle of death and rebirth in a European climate with relatively sharp fluctuations during seasons. We might speculate that geographical circumstances in different latitudes, for instance in a sub-tropical or tropical climate with a stark contrast between the dry and the wet season, would call for a reinterpretation of this particular set of myths.[40]

More pertinently, given that mortal love triangles usually do not end well in medieval Celtic imagination, perhaps successful adultery is a case of something which only pertains to Gods and not mortals, just as in the famous quote by the Catalan architect Antonio Gaudí: The straight line belongs to men and the curve to God (*la línia recta és l'home, la corba pertany a Déu*). Either way, a pleasant side effect is that a favourite insult of the alt-right is defanged once we realize that the Old Gods of western Europe were engaged in ritual adultery, and that the tradition was continued by aristocracy in many parts of western Europe, at least as reflected in its literature.[41]

Another surprising aspect of Cernunnos which is only briefly addressed in this book and which could be expanded in other publications is his androgyny, not usually acknowledged in his common interpretation and gendering as the Horned God, but in harmony with Dionysian and Shaivite themes and attested in Celtic iconography.[42] This indeed makes sense: the masculinity within Cernunnos is vast enough to encompass its opposite; ditto for his immense power which allows for cyclical periods of seeming powerlessness as well.

Within at least some hard reconstructionist circles, comparativist analogies which permeate the entire monograph are bound to provoke irritated or even irate responses and accusations of non-committal Jungianism. In response, one might wonder whether neo-Paganism, including polytheism and heathenism, would even exist without the studies by James Frazer, Georges Dumézil and Mircea Eliade, flawed as they were. Comparative studies may be several steps removed from any desired "primordial" Celtic tradition, but they are a necessary component of understanding the layers of the *interpretatio romana*, which, should be remembered, is a constant feature in all iconographic and textual materials we have. Remarkably, while many Neopagans engage with art history, there is very little mention of the rich corpus of Celtic archaeology, for instance the truly accessible works by Barry Cunliffe.

Furthermore, it must be noted that the triangle of Cernunnos-Dionysos-Śiva is one of inherited shared *prototypes*, and not externally imposed *archetypes*. Whether for strictly scholarly or devotional purposes, study and meditation on their commonly shared attributes is a fruitful endeavour. This can lead to a further reflection upon the concept of epiclesis (ἐπίκλησις) in which particular regional or other specialized attributes and epithets (ἐπίθετον) are evoked, and to what extent they could be timeless or timebound, just like the Old Norse *heiti* or the standard 108 names of Śiva, with which prayer beads can be used.[43]

Let me offer another practical suggestion by which the abyss between "hard particularist" and "soft assimilationist" practitioners could be bridged: one technique would involve engaging in acts of historically or culturally grounded "lateral devotion" and meditation upon divine Beings who share (Cernunnos-Dionysos-Śiva) or later acquire a common origin (Egyptian Aset-Roman Isis, or the axis of Bríd-Saint Brigid-Haitian Maman Brigitte). Even if one should decide in the end that they are indeed utterly distinct entities, that would be a historically and culturally informed decision, rather than just a hunch.[44]

Whether for strictly scholarly or devotional purposes, we must remain mindful of the complexity and the dynamic inherent in this maze of inherited paths which constantly diverge (as during the initial Indo-European migrations and the subsequent periods of settlement) and then again intersect and join later under vastly different historical conditions (such as the Celto-Roman political dispensation, the recasting of all narratives in a medieval Christian garb, the nineteenth century rediscovery and reanalysis of Celtic sources for political purposes, and the twentieth century post-Christian religious movements).

Perhaps the scholar and the devotee are not so different after all; both endeavours involve solar periods of joyous study and meditation as well as lunar fallow times of loneliness and agonizing doubt. Ultimately, true inspiration and intellectual precision are never opposed to each other; like the left and the right hand, they work in tandem, ideally producing that fleeting, yet magnificent state known as *imbas forosnai*.

[1] For a sense of how debates on the Gundestrup Cauldron have developed across decades, see tree seminal articles, including Phyllis Fray Bober, "Cernunnos: Origin and Transformation of a Celtic Divinity", in: *American Journal of Archaeology* 55/1 (1951), pp. 13-5; A. K. Bergquist and T. F. Taylor, "The origin of the Gundestrup cauldron", in: Antiquity 61, (1987), p.10–24, and S. Nielsen, J. Andersen, J. Baker, C. Christensen, J. Glastrup et al. "The Gundestrup cauldron: New scientific and technical investigations", in: *Acta Archaeologica* 76 (2005), p. 1–58.

[2] In the following, I put ethnicizing terms in quote marks, since they are unambiguous products of historical developments in recent centuries and have little to no biological validity or relevance to the pre-modern period. As will be known to many readers, general perception in the US is that Neopaganism is largely a "white" religion, but also that Irish Reconstructionism, Druidry and "Celtic" Wicca tend to be more inclusive and friendlier toward "people of colour" than mainstream Germanic Heathenism and its "folkish" tendencies. Accordingly, it may come as a surprise to many American devotees of Cernunnos that "Celtic" Neopagan movements in French-speaking parts of Europe often offer a mixture of defensive and potentially xenophobic "Celtic" and Christian themes which rely on nebulous visual impressions and commonplaces rather than, say, Middle Irish textuality. See Stéphane François, "Le néo-paganisme et la politique: une tentative de comprehension" in *Raisons politiques* 2007/1 (no 25), 127-142. In the wider context of history of race in America, including many instances of interracial marriage, see Noel Ignatief's *How the Irish Became White* (London, 1995), Colin G. Calloway's *White People, Indians, and Highlanders: Tribal People and Colonial Encounters in Scotland and America* (Oxford, 2008) and the influential work by Peter Linebaugh and Marcus Rediker, *The many-headed hydra: sailors, slaves, commoners, and the hidden history of the revolutionary Atlantic* (London, 2000). In other terms, apart from the simple truth that many "people of colour" in the Americas are of Irish and Scottish ancestry, we can be certain that the Lord of Beasts is rather favourable to mingling of peoples and animals and reshufflings of genes, and that from a truly Cernunnian perspective, nation borders made in the last two hundred years are mere scratchings in the mud which might disappear before long.

[3] Among the more original offerings of personal experiences, see Nicholas R. Mann, *The Dark God: A Personal Journey Through the Underworld* (St. Paul, 1996). Of interest is also Nigel Jackson, *Masks of Misrule: Horned God and His Cult in Europe* (Milverton, 1996), although the numerous spelling mistakes cry out for an editor. The most recent work by one of the editors of this volume and a practitioner, Jason Mankey, *The Horned God of the Witches* (Woodbury, 2021) is certainly to be recommended.

[4] For a much kinder rapprochement between the two worlds, see Paul Harrison, *Profane Egyptologists: The Modern Revival of Ancient Egyptian Religion* (Abingdon, 2018).

[5] Margaret Murray, The God of the Witches (London, 1931), Robert Graves, *The White Goddess: a Historical Grammar of Poetic Myth* (London, 1948). Among Jean Markale's numerous works, see especially his *Le druidisme. Traditions et dieux des Celtes* (Paris, 1985), translated into many European languages and perhaps the most articulate expression of his vision. Peter Berresford Ellis has critiqued Graves' lack of Celtic studies and in particular; see his "The Fabrication of 'Celtic' Astrology" at http://cura.free.fr/xv/13ellis2.html.

[6] For Harvard, see https://io9.gizmodo.com/the-wealthiest-university-on-earth-cant-afford-its-acad-5904601 and more recently for UC and Germany https://www.sciencemag.org/news/2019/02/university-california-boycotts-publishing-giant-elsevier-over-journal-costs-and-open.

[7] The digital edition of the *Dictionary of the Irish Language: Based Mainly on Old and*

Middle Irish Materials and the magnificent primary sources at *CELT: Corpus of Electronic Texts*, have made the "lay scholarship" possible. While a self-taught approach works fine with Irish nouns, one wonders how those researchers handle the notoriously difficult Old and Middle Irish verbal system, all the more so since it is also vastly understudied compared to its Greek analogue and often drastically simplified in short introductions to the language. For those who would delve into this, Kim McCone, *The early Irish verb* (Maynooth, 1987) remains the standard study.

[8] While individual German-speaking scholars, especially those at Marburg, Bonn and Vienna, still produce superb scholarship on questions of archaeology. linguistics and literature, there is a strong sense that the epicentres of Celtic studies have shifted from central to western Europe, and, most perniciously, there are only a select few university where medieval Celtic languages and cultures are taught. Even in Ireland itself, several academic positions for Old and Middle Irish have been eliminated. The general crisis of higher education everywhere has led to diminished output and uncertainty about the way that the academic field will reproduce. One possible path, still avoided by most professional academics, is self-publication; here, see the impeccably scholarly and yet accessible A *Student's Companion to Old Irish Grammar* (2013) by the Dutch scholar Ranke van Vries of St Xavier University in Canada. For an excellent and concise introduction into professional Celtic studies, with many bibliographies and even a section on "Neo-Paganism and modern Celtic ideology (*Keltenideologie*)", see Bernhard Müller, *Die Kelten: Geschichte, Kultur und Sprache* (Tübingen, 2015).

[9] Concerning Cernunnos, the following essay composed by Ceisiwr Serith (*a nom de plume* of an American practitioner) is often-cited in Neopagan circles. While it is remarkably thorough in its coverage of depictions of Cernunnos, the essay ultimately presents its own vision of the Celtic God as something firmly confirmed by scholarship. See https://ceisiwrserith.com/therest/Cernunnos/cernunnospaper.htm

[10] For linguistic reconstruction, see the volume by Rogério Fernandes and Steve Hansen, *Anthologia Gallica: Senobrixta-Galáthach hAthevíu Poetry and Prose* (2010) with their texts in two versions of Neo-Gaulish, acclaimed by David Stifter and Bernard Mees. A second volume was published in 2017. One author who also claims expertise in Celtic languages have contributed toward a Gaulish reconstructionist practice, see Segomâros Widugeni, *Ancient Fire: An Introduction to Gaulish Celtic Polytheism* (Tucson, AR, 2018)

[11] The abundant Neopagan literature includes David Rankine and Sorita d'Este, *The Guises of the Morrigan – The Irish Battle of Sex & Battle* (London, 2005), Stephanie Woodfield, *Celtic Lore & Spellcraft of the Dark Goddess: Invoking the Morrigan* (Woodbury, MN, 2011), Christopher Penczak's *Feast of the Morrighan* [sic] (Salem, NH, 2012), Morgan Daimler, *The Morrigan: Meeting the Great Queens* (Winchester, UK, 2014), Courtney Weber, *The Morrigan: Celtic Goddess of Magick and Might* (Newburyport, 2019). Particularly notable here is the relatively voluminous *Book of the Great Queen: The Many Faces of the Morrigan from Ancient Legends to Modern Devotions* (Oakland, CA, 2015) by Morpheus Ravenna, a much-admired martial arts instructor and a member of Coru Cothubodua priesthood, located in the San Francisco area. Except for Daimler, the authors do not quote sources in Old or Middle Irish. A devotional book with contributions by many authors, some of whom do have a professional Celticist background (for instance, the scholar known as P. Sufenas Virius Lupus, with credentials from the UK and Ireland), is also available: *By Blood, Bone and Blade: A Tribute to the Morrigan*, ed. by Nicole Bonvisuto (Conway, AR, 2014). In striking contrast, there are very few scholarly works dedicated to the Mórrígan. Neopagans often cite the Ph.D. dissertation by A. Gulermovich Epstein, "War Goddess: The Morrigan and her Germano-Celtic Counter-

parts" (UCLA, 1988) and the difficult-to-obtain monograph by Rosalind Clark, *The Great Queens: Irish Goddesses from the Morrígan to Cathleen ní Houlihan*. Also mentioned is Chapter 3 in Noémie Beck's Ph.D. dissertation, *Goddesses in Celtic Religion Cult and Mythology: A Comparative Study of Ancient Ireland, Britain and Gaul* (Lyon, 2010). Yet, the most informed scholarly monograph by the Breton scholar Christian-Joseph Guyonvarc'h and his wife Françoise Le Roux, *La souveraineté guerrière de l'Irlande: Morrigan, Bodb, Macha* (re-published at Fousnant, 2016), has not made its way into Neopagan circles, presumably because it was written in French.

[12] Most eloquently articulated by John Beckett, a Texas-based engineer and author of two insightful Neopagan books, in his enormously popular blog entry "What to do when you hear the call of the Morrigan" at https://www.patheos.com/blogs/johnbeckett/2017/07/hear-call-morrigan.html. Notably, Beckett is also a devotee of Cernunnos, with whom he works even more closely than with the Mórrígan (the categories of "working" with deities and "serving" them being derived from Afro-Caribbean traditions and popularized among Neopagan since the 1980s). The Wikipedia entry on the Mórrígan which includes a long list about her appearances in popular culture also testifies to this widespread fascination, particularly but not exclusively among people of Irish ethnic background.

[13] In German, see the third edition of *Cernunnos: Vom Schamanen zum Druiden Merlin* by Harry Eilenstein (Norderstadt, 2018), who has authored many other books on popular esoteric subjects. In French, other recent publications seemingly devoted to Cernunnos range widely from the academic monograph by Anne Lombard-Jourdan and Alexis Charniguet, *Cernunnos, dieu Cerf des Gaulois* (Paris, 2004), which in fact focuses much more on medieval French royal insignia and the patron saint of France, St. Denis, rather than on the Gaulish divinity, to other non-academic publications, including Michaël, *l'homme-cerf chez les Celtes : Cernunnos, Dieu celte, et les 7 rayons de Michaël* (Quebec, 2016) by the self-proclaimed Essene Olivier Manitara, which seeks to attract a popular audience by merging speculations about archangels with a vague Celtic component. In contrast, Gérard Poitrenaud's study *Dans les cercles de Cernunnos: Le dieu primordial des Celtes et ses avatars* (Toulouse, 2017) is more pertinent and rooted in the author's literary (though not strictly Celticist) studies, speculating that Cernunnos could be read as the "primordial phallus, the cosmic tree and the sidereal wheel." In this reading, out of the antlers of the sacrificial stag, the two antagonistic forces of the universe emerge, pulling the entire creation into an eternal hunt. As evocative as Poitrenaud's work is, his book largely represents a personal meditation and perhaps somewhat of a reaction to *Cernunnos, le dioscure sauvage*, rather than an exploration of original textual or material sources.

[14] The word "savage" in English originates in medieval Norman French *sauvage* (andultimately from the Latin silvaticus), but the two words differ slightly in their connotation. My English translation of the term as "wild" rather than the more derogatory "savage" is more appropriate to the French original.

[15] Ossetic exerts a fascination upon many Indo-Europeanist scholars, as the almost sole remnant of an Iranian continuum between Hungary and the Pamirs, and the only living Iranian language which did not experience a strong hegemonic pull of linguistically related Persian-Dari because of its remote location. Although the written tradition was only established in the nineteenth century, Ossetic possesses a rich mythological lore which may in part harken back to nomadic Scythian and Sarmatian traditions. See André Sikojev, *Die Narten. Söhne der Sonne. Mythen und Heldensagen der Skythen, Sarmaten und Osseten* (Köln 1985).

[16] Patrice Lajoye, *Des Dieux Gaulois: Petits essais de mythologie* (Budapest, 2008), p. 30. For visual depictions of Cernunnos, also see Simone Deyts, *Images des dieux de la Gaule* (Paris, 1992), particularly p. 36-45. For the standard discussion in English, see Miranda Green, Animals in Celtic Life and Myth (London, 1992).

[17] Claude Sterckx, Taranis, *Sucellos et quelques autres: le dieu souverain des Celtes, de la Gaule à l'Irlande* (Brussels, 2005), especially volume III, chapter LII on Cernunnos, p. 461-492.

[18] Bernard Sergent, L*e livre des dieux: Tome II, Celtes et Grecs* (Paris, 2004).

[19] As Sergent exclaimed to the authors in his initial assessment, a deer is obviously not a fish; yet, as he continues, this "beautiful and big study" must be read, allowing the authors to guide us. CDS, p.17f.

[20] CDS, p.22.

[21] Daniélou's moral qualities are mentioned here since they deeply affected and marred his scholarship. Similarly to Carlos Castaneda, he combined his academic expertise with numerous unsubstantiated speculations about pre-historical past in order to further his vision of an ideal hierarchical and racialist society, see Alain Daniélou, *Shiva et Dionysos, la religion de la nature et de l'eros, de la préhistoire à l'avenir* (Paris, 1979). The scholarly debate has been resumed recently by Bernard Sergent in *Le Dieu Fou: Essai sur les origines de Siva et de Dionysos* (Paris, 2016), to be recommended instead. For Cernunnos, see p. 393-400.

[22] Joseph Campbell, *The Masks of God, vol. IV: Creative Mythology* (London, 1968), p.410-412; Glenys Goetinck, "Indian Parallels and Belgic Influences on Medieval Welsh Literature", in: Ollodagos, VIII (1995), p.157-182.

[23] CDS, throughout the books and specifically II.1, II.2 and II.3, and especially IV.2. and VI.3. Note that I will cite topics by listing sections rather than page numbers in order to avoid numerous mentions of passim and idem.

[24] Jean-Jacques Hatt, *Mythes et dieux de la Gaule. Les grandes divinités masculines* (Paris, 1989), Vol.I, p.71-93 .Volume II (1995) was made freely available on the internet by Hatt's family after his death, see jeanjacqueshatt.free.fr/01-tome-2-mythes-et-dieux-texte-seul.pdf

[25] Somewhat amusingly, Lugh is much less well-known and frequented in polytheist circles than Cernunnos, but, most likely for textual reasons, the situation is reversed among scholars. See the Ph.D. dissertation by Krista L. Ovist, "The integration of Mercury and Lugus: Myth and history in late Iron Age and early Roman Gaul" (University of Chicago, 2004).

[26] CDS, section III.2. Indeed, putting the V sign behind someone's head during a photo session might spell victory to an unsuspecting American, but it can have severe physical consequences in many parts of the Mediterranean, as this form of "temporary antlers" immediately signifies adultery.

[27] CDS, III.1 and III.2.

[28] One would expect to find a subchapter about Noísi mac Usnig and Derdriu, since Noísi was also a famed hunter. However, Fergus mac Róich is suggested as yet another face of Cernunnos.

[29] For the etymology of the roots of these names, see Xavier Delamarre, *Dictionnaire de la Langue Gauloise, Une approche linguistique du vieux celtique continental*. Paris, 2003, rendering -smero, -smerto as caretaker, even foresighted one, p. 277; for the many attempts to interpret *lugus*, p.211; Cernunnos can be found on p.106 within the discussion of the root *carnon*, which means both horn and trumpet. Also see Ranko Matasović, *Etymological Dictionary of Proto-Celtic* (Leiden, 2009), p.190f. For the epigraphic record, see http://db.edcs.eu/epigr/epi_einzel.php?s_sprache=en&p_belegstelle=CIL+13%2C+03026&r_sortierung=Belegstelle

[30] Crucially confirmed by Diodoros Sikeliotes in his Bibliotheca historica (*Βιβλιοθήκη ἱστορική*), IV. CDS

[31] For details of the argument, see the entire chapter II. For attestations of Cernunnos in toponomy, see Jacques Lacroix, *Les noms d'origine Gauloise, La Gaule des dieux* (Paris, 2007) p.98-101.

[32] CDS, IV.3.1 and VI.2.

[33] CDS, VI, 3.

[34] For the young Cernunnos, see CDS., IV.2; for Dylan, see II.3; for Maponos, III.5. For dogs and wolves in Celtic literatures, see Phillip A. Bernhardt-House, *Werewolves, magical hounds, and dog-headed men in Celtic literature : a typological study of shape-shifting* (Lewiston, NY, 2010).

[35] See the comparative chart in CDS, p.490.

[36] Bernard Robreau, "Les Celtes et le chamanisme", *Ollodagos*, XXII (2008), p.195-277.

[37] CDS, p. 429.

[38] Alexei Kondratiev, *The Apple Branch: A Path to Celtic Ritual* (New York, 2003). Certainly the sales of this book would make most scholars green with envy, as it went through at least six editions.

[39] For such a minimalist approach, see M. Altjohann, "Cernunnos?" in: *Dieux des Celtes. Götter der Kelten. Gods of the Celts*, edited by Ch. M. Ternes and H. Zinser (Luxemburg, 2002), p.149-181.

[40] For instance, could this dynamic apply to Wsjr (Osiris) as the God of fertile, green land and Swtḫ (Sutekh/Seth as the God of the arid, red desert, with Nbt-ḥwt (Nephthys) and even ꜣst (Isis) playing the part of the contested Goddess? Some of those questions are explored in my ongoing work on Swtḫ as a Neopagan deity of queerness and anarchism. For the prime example of an academic monograph which has influenced an entire current of occult and Neopagan thought, see H. Te Velde, *Seth, God of Confusion: A Study of His Role in Egyptian Mythology and Religion* (Leiden, 1967)

[41] Then again, those self-appointed defenders of the western civilization are not known

for studying Indo-European linguistics or for cultivating subtlety or playfulness. For a scholarly work on this topic, see Peggy McCracken, *The Romance of Adultery: Queenship and Sexual Transgression in Old French Literature* (Philadelphia, 1998). Incidentally, another topic which is never addressed by nativist Neopagans who elevate an abstract and supposedly unproblematic "northern European" heritage is the substantial number of Irish and Scottish slaves in Iceland, resulting in one of the largest slave revolts in Europe in 875, when Hjörleifr Hróðmarsson was killed by his thralls, see Sigfus M. Johnsen, *Saga Vestmannaeyja* (Reykjavik, 1946). Both of those instances indicate the importance of research beyond Wikipedia.

[42] CDS, IV, 2.

[43] Within the Abrahamic tradition, the practice on meditating upon 99 divine attributes is particularly well established in Islam, where they are called "the beautiful names" (al-'asma' al-husna). The famous Sufi Ibn 'Arabī (d.1240), one of the greatest minds of his time, whose tolerance of other traditions and unusual perspectives on angels led to accusations of pantheism, wrote an insightful treatise on divine names. For a critical edition and translation from Arabic into French, see Pablo Beneito, *Les secrets des noms de Dieu* (Beirut, 2010). The treatise is cited here not as a nudge toward Abrahamic teachings, but rather as a meditational technique which goes far beyond mere praise and enumerations, encouraging the seeker to emulate and acquire the qualities evoked by each of the names.

[44]Those who are so inclined might also reflect upon the manifold historical processes during which the regional ancestral God of Abraham and his family branched out into his universalizing Jewish, Christian and Islamic manifestations. But to return to Celtic divine onomastics, one may consult the articles in Wolfgang Spickermann, ed. *Keltische Götternamen als individuelle Option?* (Rahden, 2013), and Andreas Hofender, Patrizia de Bernardo Stempel, eds.*Théonymie celtique, cultes, interpretatio / Keltische Theonymie, Kulte, interpretatio* (Vienna, 2013).

Selected bibliography (please also refer to endnotes):

Altjohann, Michael. "Cernunnos?" In *Dieux des Celtes. Götter der Kelten. Gods of the Celts,* edited by Charles M. Ternes and Hartmut Zinser. (Luxemburg: Association européenne pour l'étude scientifique des religions, 2002), 149-181.

Deyts, Simone. *Images des dieux de la Gaule.* Paris: Éditions Errance, 1992.

François, Stéphane. "Le néo-paganisme et la politique: une tentative de comprehension," *Raisons politiques* 1, no.25 (2007): 127-142.

Goetinck, Glenys. "Indian Parallels and Belgic Influences on Medieval Welsh Literature," *Ollodagos* VIII (1995): 157-182.

Gricourt, Daniel and Dominique Hollard. *Cernunnos, le dioscure sauvage: Recherches comparatives sur la divinité dionysiaque des Celtes.* Paris: L'Harmattan, 2010.

Hatt, Jean-Jacques. *Mythes et dieux de la Gaule I. Les grandes divinités masculines.* Paris: Éditions Picard, 1989.

Lacroix, Jacques. *Les noms d'origine Gauloise, La Gaule des dieux.* Paris: Éditions Errance,

2007.

Lajoye, Patrice. *Des Dieux Gaulois: Petits essais de mythologie*. Budapest: Archaeolingua, 2008.

Müller, Bernhard. *Die Kelten: Geschichte, Kultur und Sprache*. Tübingen: Francke, 2015.

Nielsen, S. and J. Andersen, J. Baker, C. Christensen, J. Glastrup et al. "The Gundestrup cauldron: New scientific and technical investigations," *Acta Archaeologica* 76 (2005): 1–58.

Robreau, Bernard. "Les Celtes et le chamanisme," *Ollodagos* XXII (2008):195-277.

Sergent, Bernard. *Le Dieu Fou: Essai sur les origines de Siva et de Dionysos*. Paris: Les Belles Lettres, 2016.

Part 2

Meeting Cernunnos

Cernunnos and Me
Kirk S. Thomas

Back when I was just a little kid, maybe 8 years old or so, my family spent the summer at my grandmother's old house south of Salt Lake City, Utah. This house sat at the base of Mt. Olympus (I kid you not) in the Wasatch Mountains. Coming from Washington State, I had no friends in Salt Lake, and spent most of my time alone, playing in the overgrown couple of acres behind the house. It was a wonderful and wild place back there, and I loved it. But one day something strange happened. While playing back there by myself I suddenly felt like someone, or some thing, was watching me. It was a spooky feeling, and very strong, and I remember that the hairs on my head stood up. I had a sudden 'knowing' that whatever it was, it wanted something from me, so I ran into the house and rummaged in the refrigerator until I found some grapes. I took them out to the wild area and found a rock back there to lay them on. And then I fled back into the house, because, frankly, I was quite frightened.

The next day the grapes were gone.

I had no idea who or what that was back there, but the experience certainly got my attention.

Religion wasn't mentioned in my house when I was growing up. My parents had managed to get themselves excommunicated from the Mormon Church before I was born, and they wanted nothing to do with any of it. Christmas was about Santa Claus and presents, and Easter was about eggs and bunnies. I was vaguely aware that there was a big religion out there connected with these two holidays, but the details were pretty sketchy. And, frankly, I couldn't care less.

I did have a flirtation with witchcraft in my late teens, thanks to reading Sybil Leek and Paul Huson, but it didn't survive college. I was your basic agnostic (practically atheist) man for most of my life. I hate to admit it, but I was one of those tiresome people who always said that he was not religious, just spiritual, as though I had any idea about what that meant.

At the age of 47 I changed my life completely. I split from my ex and moved back to the USA from the UK, essentially starting my life over again. I tried all sorts of new experiences, with a new partner, and one of these was BDSM. The catharsis that I experienced in that first year helped clear out a lot of the deadwood in my soul, which opened me up to experiencing something new, something that would change my life even more.

It was the needle play that did it. I had started out receiving a couple of needles in my chest, just to see if I could do it, and then moved up to 35 needles in one go. It was the third time, when I was determined to get 99 needles in one session, that it happened.

We were at around 65 needles or so when suddenly it was as though the Heavens opened above me. I was suddenly aware that there were figures coming into view that were not there before. My vision became layered, as though one reality were sitting on top of another one. I could still see my partner putting in the needles and the room was quite clear, but these 'others' were appearing on top of them, as though they were superimposed. Neither layer was completely solid - they both seemed to bleed through into the other. And I had no idea who these figures were.

The first to appear was a lovely woman with dark hair who was suddenly standing on my left side as I lay on the table. There was also a dark and rather scary looking woman at my feet with her back to me. Some male figures also appeared around that scary woman and I was struggling to understand what was going on.

And then He appeared. On my right side there was a beautiful, naked man with antlers growing out of his head. Good Gods, I knew who this was! Cernunnos, the god of the witches that I had seen pictures of back in my teenage days. And He looked at me closely and said something like, "Close enough. Have I finally gotten your attention now?" And He gave me an amused and knowing smile. Later I would come to understand that He appeared naked to me because He knew me well enough to know that His nudity would certainly get my attention. Since that time He has always appeared to me dressed.

So who, exactly, was this god? I knew so little about Him. I ransacked all the books I could find, and discovered that He is usually referred to as a god of the forest (and animals?), part man and part stag, perhaps also a god of prosperity (thanks to all those purses depicted in His carvings and the torcs He holds). Being half man and half stag implies, to me, that He is a liminal being. He is neither man nor beast and perhaps is both, all at the same time. And if He was the Being that I sensed as a child, He would have also been in a liminal location. Those overgrown two acres behind my grandmother's house were not a forest, by any means. Nor were they part of cultivated earth. Rather, they were somewhere in between the wild slopes of Mt. Olympus and the very human houses and gardens on Holladay Boulevard.

On the Gundestrup Cauldron He is depicted with a dog, a symbol of the Underworld, so might He also be a god of the dead? And if so, perhaps He is also a god of the riches of the Underworld, of silver, gold, and, yes, oil? Caesar referred to a Gaulish god, often assumed to be Cernunnos, by the Roman name of Dis Pater, which roughly translates as 'Father of Riches', at least according to Cicero. And from there it would be an easy step to go from the riches of the Underworld to god of the dead.

So my UPG tells me that Cernunnos, my Patron, is a Lord of Liminality, Lord of Prosperity, and a god of those places in between the wild and the tame, sort of like the Roman god Silvanus, who protected the boundaries of the fields. He is also a god of the Underworld and of the riches under the earth.

Here at the White Mountain Druid Sanctuary at Trout Lake Abbey, I have set about creating a sacred enclosure of shrines to my gods. There is a large stone circle and a building I call the Sanctuary, where I can hold smaller public rites in the winter when the stone circle is filled in with snow. The shrines are still being built, but completed so far are shrines to the Dagda, the Morrigan, a temporary one to Taranis (to go with his massive stone pillar) and one to the god Lugh.

But the latest shrine to be built is to Cernunnos. It sits on the East-West axis that runs through the center of the stone circle, and it is at the west end. I placed it there because the west is the direction of the

lands of the dead in ancient Irish Celtic culture. And I am currently starting a shrine to Brigit and Fire at the eastern end of that axis.

There is an icon of the god in the center wall of the shrine and there
are antlers attached to the roof line. Two signs (for visitors who have
no idea about the gods) are in place, one describing who Cernunnos is,
and another with a prayer to Him that people can read. Under the icon
there is a cabinet holding a fire stick and incense, and on top of it is a
bowl to hold the burning incense. There is a fire altar before the shrine
and a bench behind that for meditation and contemplation of the icon.

I make use of my shrines in two ways, depending on what I am doing.
The normal, daily use is to stand before the icon, light a piece of incense
as an offering, and speak a prayer to the god in humility and reverence.
But occasionally I stand before a shrine and do a full ritual. I place charcoal in the fire altar to take my offerings and perform the rite to Him in
the nude, when possible. I do this because I want Them to see that I have
nothing to hide, and come to Them as I am. Since the Abbey is a public
place, this can be difficult to arrange, so I tend to do these rites at night
when visitors aren't about. But I make offerings to the god through the
fire, such as food and whiskey, sharing between myself and Him. And
then I take time to go deep into trance and to commune with Him before closing up the rite. Should any visitors wish to do something like this
at any of the shrines they are more than welcome to do so (well, probably without the nudity part), as long as they bring their own offerings
or make a donation to allow us to buy more. I will provide the charcoal.
And I would love to see someone take advantage of the shrines in this way.

Hail Cernunnos!
God of the Forest,
God of the Underworld,
God of Liminality,
We praise You!

You who sits between the Living and Dead,
You who stands between the Wild and Tame,
You who guards the wealth of our Ancestors,
We call to You!

Lord of In-Between,
Keeper of the Gates between the Worlds,
Lord of Animals, Lord of the Wilds,
We make offerings to You!

May our lives be prosperous,
May we truly know ourselves,
May we make a difference in the World.
Cernunnos, accept our offerings!

Cernunnos Shrine – Trout Lake Abbey
Shrine built by Kirk Thomas. Photo by John Beckett

Encounter with The Stag God
Kris Hughes

Some years ago, I was in a period of spending a lot of time meditating and trying to deepen my practice. I had even been lucky enough to have some of my first encounters with deities. One of my meditation techniques was to take myself to a room, outside this reality, which had a set of French windows which opened into a forest garden. I had been using a different method when I had encountered deities, so I wasn't expecting to meet anyone there. However, in He came. The stag god that I think of as Cernunnos, or Herne.

His arrival was sudden. Initially He stood upright like a man. This seemed natural to him, without the forced balance that a large animal has when standing on its hind legs. His head, body, and face were those of a stag, yet there was something anthropomorphic about His appearance: a suggestion of woolen clothing, like a jacket. In the vision I was also standing, and immediately He embraced me, and the protruding ribcage of His animal chest, and the slight awkwardness of His hooved forelimbs were very noticeable. There was also a strong feeling of physical and emotional warmth.

The thought that formed in my mind was, "He is my father. This is my father." This moment ended all too soon, and He resumed the shape of a normal stag, seeming to grow larger and larger once He left through the open doors and disappeared into the night. When I considered this vision later, I felt that my sense of this stag god had a flavor of my own father about Him. I was pleased to have had the experience, which felt healing at a time in my life when I was a bit lonely and wretched, but it didn't seem to be calling me to take action or bringing me any clear message.

Around this time, I was working on creating a deck of oracle cards, and trying to engage deeply with the different plants, animals, and other entities which I was including. This involved doing deep meditation work on each card, plus delving into my personal memories and experiences, reading folklore, natural history, and mythology. At the same time, I was doing experimental readings with them for some volunteers, who were also cartomancers, and who were giving me feedback. From this process, I was distilling an essence which was meaningful to me, concerning each card.

One of these cards was The Red Stag. (I should probably clarify that I'm referring to the animal whose scientific name is *Cervus elephas* - which in Europe we call red deer, and in North America is called elk.) My sense of this card was still a work in progress, when it came up in a reading for one of my volunteers. Due to this person's query, a great deal about this card became clear, as it concerned difficulties in the relationship between two obsessively creative individuals. At the same time, my encounter with Cernunnos also began to make more sense to me.

Over time I've come to see The Red Stag as representing a form of fatherhood and therefore a deep creative impulse. A primal urge to make something, to bring forth a representation of one's deepest being as a gift to the future. In nature, the stag is an animal preoccupied with breeding, and with fighting to breed. When we try to transpose that directly into human behaviour he doesn't sound like a very nice guy. But if we think of the creative urge, it might mean an incredibly strong urge to make something meaningful, or to pass on something important. This is a form of fatherly love, too, although it's not the directly nurturing, caring and protective love of a mother, or even of many modern fathers. It could be the love of an artist or other creative person for their work, and ultimately for the society who will benefit in some way from that work. It could be the love of an activist, as they strive to create a better world for the future, or of a researcher, or civil engineer. This kind of creative urge can sometimes make people difficult or selfish in their personal lives even though they are driven by love.

Because we live in a society that is steeped in Christian beliefs and expectations, even as Pagans we often want our deities to be interested in our personal feelings and daily lives in the same way that the Christian god has been portrayed in the last century. If you have a very close relationship with Cernunnos, then I suppose that kind of relationship is possible, but generally I suspect that He is a better choice to call on if you hope to produce some great body of work, or to fight for a cause like saving the natural world from destruction. Acts of primal creation, of immense effort, perhaps at great personal cost.

One final thing which I have come to understand about the Stag God is that if you scratch the surface you will find a fine balance of male and female energy within. If we consider the animal, stags are only in their uber-male state of rut for less than two months of the year. Once they shed their antlers in winter, they look much like hinds, except for being a bit larger. They combine their immense power and stamina with the same graceful movement and delicate legs as the females, presenting a gentle, more feminine aspect which speaks to me of that male/female balance. This is something that we could use more of today, both as individuals and as a culture. The macho man and the helpless female are stereotypes we desperately need to leave behind, both in our wider society and in things like Pagan art.

My personal experience of the Stag God has been enriched by these different aspects of strongly driven creativity and an acknowledgement of the importance of keeping male and female energy in balance within myself. It has taught me to recognize that these things tend to be cyclical, and to accept that. I'm grateful for my glimpse of The Stag God, which has strengthened and encouraged me often, when I have struggled to keep going on a difficult path.

Silence
Jay Clark

In silence, he came to me. I was not looking for him, and yet he came. He sat with me in the silence, long before we ever said a word to each other. Born and raised in the panhandle of Oklahoma, I lived not in an area filled with trees, but with the plains and endless open sky that revealed a delicious plethora of stars each night. I would travel to a small canyon a small ways from my backyard. I would stand on the edge and slightly lean into the endless winds and be filled with such peace. He was there with me. Silence.

At the bottom of that small ravine was a tiny patch of trees, in which I loved to play. It was there that I encountered snakes, quail, horned lizards and spy the occasional coyote who ventured out during the day. I knew nothing of Paganism, old nor new. And yet I made a shrine there. That small grove felt sacred to me and I wanted to honor it in some way. In that tender wildness, he sat with me, never speaking.

He was with me as I moved into puberty, my body producing hair in various places, and the newfound pleasures of exploring my own body. It was guys like him that first opened my eyes that I might not be like other guys in my attractions. It wrestled with him like Jacob and his angel in the Bible until I finally made peace with that side of myself. I felt his touch in my first kiss, my first lovemaking, feral and yet tender.

I first learned of him in college and heard him called in a gathering. I had no interest in him. He was too manly, I thought. What would one such as he want with a gay guy? In my shame, I ran from him, into the arms of the Mother.

He stood with me as I held the hand of my husband of sixteen years as he breathed his last breath and succumbed to cancer. He was the Lord of Shadows and the Hunter who teaches that death too is part of life. It was there that I first allowed myself to see him much more fully and not flinch away as if I were not man enough for him.

Now, we sit in silence together again. More often than not among the trees or next to a stream. But we talk, now too. I leave offerings to him and ask his blessings and help. I feel his voice guide and teach me as I work to make this world a little better place. He is my God. He is nature, life, death, and all these things in-between. He is the joy of dancing, the laughter in my song, and the silent sorrow of loss. He is nature. We speak now, god to priest. He is my life and god, Cernunnos.

Blessings of the Horned One
Damh the Bard

Late Spring 2002

My sandaled feet touched warm soil as I walked through the Sussex woodland. Evening was falling but light still reached through the spring-green leaves above and painted the woodland floor with a dappled array of gold and silver. I raised the flute to my lips and played to the Spirits of Place as we walked along the footpath, deeper into the forest.

Tonight was an important night for the Grove. Two initiations beckoned. Moments of magic during which we would witness two souls exclaim to the trees, the animals, the Gods, the Universe, that they were ready - place the honey upon their tongues, ignite the fire in their heads, show them the poetry written upon the land, open the Gates of Annwn and let them see the wonders of the Otherworld as they step upon the same path as Merlin, Taliesin, Amergin. Ferns quivered, animals watched, birds sang, as we made our way to the Sacred Grove.

Soon, dusk fell. The two were led away and each asked to sit by a tree, alone, and wait to be brought to the circle. Time spent in contemplation, in the quiet peace of the forest. The circle was cast, the Spirits of the Elements called, the Awen invoked.

This is not the place to write of ceremony. What passed between us that night will remain hidden, between those who were there, but there is one moment I do wish to share. As I looked into the eyes of one of those brought to the circle, I noticed movement within the forest behind them. In the dark shadows of the trees something was moving, walking. I moved my gaze to that liminal space between Grove and trees, and there, just visible, was a figure, standing, watching. Tall, well built, eyes shining like fire. And upon the figure's head two magnificent antlers reached to the sky. No words. No more movement. Just fiery eyes watching, observing.

Magicians say that if you work magic, don't be surprised when it works. And thus when you work ceremony within the woods don't be surprised if you draw the attention of the Fair Folk, of those who live in their worlds, but whose worlds overlap with ours. And just like piercing the veil with one tiny dot of light will still attract moths, so ritual and magic attracts those who know and feel the powers with which we work within our circles. There, on the edge of our circle stood a figure I had known since childhood. And here words fail me.

How to describe the awe, the blessing, the feelings I had in that moment? I simply cannot.

I looked back to the eyes of the waiting initiate.

"We are being watched," I said. "The Horned One is here."

Sussex - 1974

I was nine years old, laying in bed, listening to the noise coming from the TV program my parents were watching downstairs. It sounded amazing. I slipped out of bed, and crept downstairs. I had discovered long ago that I could sit on the stairs unnoticed and see the TV. My parents were watching a film, an old horror film, made by Hammer from 1968 called *The Devil Rides Out*, based on an equally old Dennis Wheatley novel of the same name. I had arrived on the stairs just as Christopher Lee had stumbled upon a 'Black Mass', hence the commotion and noise. As I watched, the camera panned across and there it caught the image of a goat footed and headed figure, sitting upon a rock.

I distinctly remember my feelings. I was a little scared, of course, but not a "crikey I have to run away" kind of scared. Even in that nine year old mind I couldn't see that image as the Devil. In my admittedly short life in Sunday School I couldn't remember one passage from the Bible where the Devil is described as having cloven hoof and horn. No, there was something else going on here, and that memory has remained with me to this day as the moment my heart began to beat in rhythm with another drum. A Pagan drum.

April 1984

Popular culture made that Pagan heart beat a little faster when I first encountered Herne. It was on the old TV show *Robin of Sherwood* where

Robin was portrayed as Herne's son, and every so often he would meet Herne within Sherwood Forest. Every Sunday night our family would sit down together and watch Robin of Sherwood. I still get nostalgic when I hear Clannad's "The Hooded Man" song to this day. It dawned on me that, just as the Greeks had their Pan, so this little island also had its folklore of a Horned God, and that Horned God was not evil, was not really anything to do with Christianity at all. I had been told lies. Here was something altogether different, and once that Path revealed itself, I began to walk. I had encountered at an early age the image of who I would later know as Pan, then in my teens Herne had made himself known to me, both through popular media. I don't suppose either Richard Carpenter nor Hammer Films ever thought their stories would inspire a young man to explore magic and Paganism, but that is what happened. Add to that the music of Black Sabbath and Led Zeppelin and my teenage self found his home. But what of Cernunnos?

Glastonbury 1990

Driving home from a weekend in Glastonbury I slid the cassette into the car stereo. The farmland of the west country passed by and I listened as these words were sung:

Cernunnos, Horned One,
Cernunnos, King of the Sun,
Herne the hunted, and hunter,
Stag God of the Earth.

I knew Herne, I knew Pan, but this was the first time I had heard the name Cernunnos. Herne the hunted, and hunter they sang. So was Cernunnos a different aspect of Herne? The books at the time suggested this to be the case, as they also suggested that all Gods were one God, all Goddesses, one Goddess. I had arrived in Paganism from Ceremonial Magic so this was all quite new to me. For many years this influenced how I felt about Pan, Herne and Cernunnos. To me they were the different faces and aspects of the same God. Pan, the wildness; Herne the mystic, the hunter; Cernunnos, the Shaman/Otherworldly God of rebirth. It worked for me at the time, and my relationship with Old Horny developed from that place. This was expressed in one of my own lyrics in the second Pagan song I ever wrote called On the Noon of the Solstice where I sing:

I'm the Horned God I'm the face in the trees,
I'm the breath of the wind that rustles the leaves,
I'm the Green Man in the Wildwood I roam,
Cernunnos, I'm Pan, and I'm Herne.

I suppose we can talk theology for days. I've heard it said that Cernunnos is a title. Like Morrigan (Great Queen), and Dagda (Good God), Cernunnos' meaning is said to be 'Horned One', and the name Horned One can be ascribed to both Herne and Pan. But then there are others who have individual relationships with all three as distinct and separate Gods, and of course they are - the Greeks didn't ever call Pan, Cernunnos. Herne, in his home of Windsor Great Forest was Herne, not Cernunnos. But although I no longer see them as aspects of one God, the chorus of Noon of the Solstice still rings true for me, and can be sung honouring all three.

Present Day

My love of myth is deep. I adore the tales of *Y Mabinogi* and the Gods, Goddesses and Heroes held therein, but I always seem to come back to the Earth Goddess and the Horned God. They have been a constant in my spiritual life for decades. My relationship with Horned Gods still acknowledges those early experiences with Pan, the wildness; Herne the mystic, the hunter; Cernunnos, the Shaman/Otherworldly God of rebirth. It was the Horned One that took my hand all those years ago as a nine year old child. It was the Horned One who led me through the forest and placed my hands upon my guitar once more. It was the Horned One who came to witness the initiations that night in Sussex, and who continues to watch over me in my life. He has taught me the mysticism and wonder of the Divine Masculine, and at a time when it is so important to reassess our relationship with what it means to be a man, and to discard the things we have been taught that have led to issues with toxic masculinity, this relationship is more important than ever.

I have been told by many people that my song "Antlered Crown and Standing Stone" has helped them heal their relationship with men. That the words have helped them to open more to the Divine Masculine with trust, and an open heart.

I am lover I am Father, I am Horned God and King,
I'm the life in all of Nature, that is reborn every Spring,
Call of stag and cry of eagle, I am Child of Barleycorn,
And I am the Antlered Crown and Standing Stone.

There are times when it is hard to write a song, but that chorus just fell onto the page, as if it wanted to be written.

Late Spring 2002

The circle uncast we made our way back through the woodland. Night had fallen but we knew the way well. We walked together in silence. The two new initiates could look forward to a night of Otherworldly dreams, and a future of magic and wonder. Tomorrow, when they opened their eyes, they would see the world for the first time through the eyes of poets, and thus a new Journey would begin.

One decided to return to the place of their initiation the next night. They phoned to tell me what had happened. As they walked and reminisced about the ritual the previous night their eyes had fallen upon a shape upon the earth.

A stag antler lay in the sunlight.
In the place where the figure had stood the night before.
Watching.
Observing.

A Crown of Tines
Asa West

In the first dream, we have all cut off our antlers. It's a routine practice, like shaving one's face or legs; beauty standards are strict enough that letting one's antlers grow out would garner strange looks on the street. One young man, though, has let his grow to their full height, and he walks among us with a glorious crown of tines. He is friendly and easy-going and there is not one person among our friends who dislikes him. In my waking life, he is known for his quiet and disciplined spiritual practice. In the dream, I admire him and then go to a mirror. I should let mine grow out, too, *I think, fingering the spots on my head where I apply the razor.* Yes, I think. Yes. I'm going to grow out my antlers. *I'll be seen as an eccentric, I know, but my friend's antlers are so beautiful, so regal, that I don't care.*

I was nineteen years old when I had this dream, and had practiced my craft for only three years. Wicca in the 90's was so solidly Goddess-oriented that the Horned God sometimes seemed like a footnote in her sacred drama, the bit player who enables her to perform her work of birthing the world. I was so relieved and ecstatic to meet the sacred feminine that at first, I didn't consciously hear his low and insistent call. It took me years to truly understand the significance of my dream.

Ask a new or young witch who Cernunnos is in his own right, and they might say, "he is the god of forests and animals, of course." "And what does this title mean?" you might press. "What does it mean to be a god of forests and animals? What does it mean to be called to service by such a god?" The young witch may study you, hesitant and unsure, working out what answer they think you want to hear. "It means you love nature," they might venture. "It means you care for the earth and see it as sacred."

That answer is correct, of course. But it is also superficial, only a faint echo of the Horned One's mysteries. If one lives their entire life seeing Cernunnos as the god of forests and animals, then they can live a rich, ethical life. If they go deeper, though—if they follow his lead into the mossy labyrinths and hidden groves—they open themselves to the shattering wisdom of the unseen world.

A teacher of traditional craft once told me that true gnosis of a deity will always reveal surprises. If one has read books and looked at pictures, if one's mind holds a static and predictable image of a god, and it is exactly that form that the god takes in vision or dream, then the seeker hasn't yet broken through their preconceptions and the gnosis is incomplete. It is in this spirit that I wonder: why, out of all the gods of magic and witchcraft and the living earth, is it Cernunnos who has risen to prominence? How has this quiet, almost-forgotten god, seated with his serpent and torc in a scattered collection of artifacts, taken his place at the center of modern witchcraft? Those tempted to answer this question by plodding through history, citing Fortune and Gardner and the rest, forget that a god's rise is never inevitable. It could have been any number of gods who took the hand of the Goddess and became her consort. But instead, Cernunnos broke through. Cernunnos appeared in our dreams; Cernunnos placed the crown of tines on our heads. This is no small thing.

In *Craft of the Untamed*, Nicholaj de Mattos Frisvold observes that the title Cernunnos shares the root KRN (meaning power or elevation) with the words *corona* (crown), *karneios* (power), and *keraunos* (thunderbolt). [i] The crown, of course, is traditionally a symbol of victory and divine will, with the golden circlet on the brow of a monarch echoing the halos of Christian demigods. "We see an interesting theme surfacing related to horns or crown," Frisvold writes, "for it is at the summit the lightning is most likely to strike." [ii] In this light, Cernunnos's horns or antlers serve as a kind of divine lightning rod, enabling the transmittal of wisdom from the vastness of the stars. No wonder so many witchcraft traditions have come to see Cernunnos as a solar deity, born at midwinter and maturing at midsummer, channeling the sun's radiance to his devotees:

Cernunnos, Horned One,
Cernunnos, God of the Sun
Herne the Hunter and Hunted
Stag God of the Earth [iii]

Raven Grimassi writes that the image of the moon shining through tree branches can serve as a bridge of antlers on which the Goddess descends to her devotees.[iv] When we follow Cernunnos's winding path, when we embody the wild Horned One, we transform ourselves into vessels of divinity. We root ourselves in the rich earth and draw down the cosmos.

In some strands of traditional witchcraft, the Bucca—a Cornish deity, usually horned but often antlered, whom many practitioners recognize as Cernunnos under a local guise[v]—brings the light of knowledge and holy power in a more roundabout way. "The Horned One is held as witch-deity in chief in most 'Old Craft' recensions and expressions, and as the very initiator of the Cunning Path itself," writes Gemma Gary, describing the deity as "the very embodiment of the land mysteries and the spirit of nature."[vi] At the Horned One's heart "we find the resolving of all opposites, the traditional candle betwixt the horns symbolizing the light of 'All-Wisdom', and the mystic state of 'One-Pointedness' which is the ultimate goal of the witch and is the light that illumines the Cunning Path."[vii] In the heart of nature, then—in the depths of the soil and the muck of the land, the deepest aquifer spring and the darkest thicket—we find Cernunnos's hidden light.

And it is no accident that Cernunnos's power lies precisely in the resolving of opposites. The liminal is a place of magic and transformation: the spell worked at the crossroads, the thinning of the veil in eldritch twilight. Cernunnos is both human and animal and, therefore, neither; in pulling the witch out of the safety of rigid, civilized reality, he opens the mind to the deeper possibilities of the wildwood. Cernunnos lures us back to the genetic crossroads at which *Homo sapiens* diverged from other species, and once there, he unlocks the ancestral knowledge that predates even our most ancient human ancestors. Cernunnos leads us back to the source of all life and crowns us with the light of sacred truth: that all is one, and the power of creation is our own power.

#

I am standing on the roof of my apartment building, praying to the stars. I feel alienated in this city of concrete and asphalt, with air browned by pollution and flora parched by drought. Despairing, I close my eyes and speak to Cernunnos. "Are you here?" I ask. "Give me a sign that you're here."

I open my eyes and they immediately fall on an erect pipe, about a foot long, protruding from the neighbor's roof. I have to laugh. Often Cernunnos is subtle. Other times, he is quite blunt.

#

Another dream. I am on the shore of a river and there is a ferry waiting for me. As I approach the gangway, I see two marble statues, smiling and gesturing for me to board. They do not move, but I know that they see me, that their smiles and gestures are for me. These statues are a god and goddess, nameless but divine nonetheless, and I shiver at the enormity of the encounter. I board the boat and it disembarks. In the front, behind the wheel, I catch a glimpse of a body that is green and sinewy like living wood. I know Cernunnos is sailing this ship, but I wake before I find out what awaits me on the other shore.

#

Cernunnos, regardless of his original function, is now a god of sex to many of his devotees: consort of the Goddess, spirit of the rutting stag, keeper of the bliss of orgasm. But sex is so much more than pleasure or even fertility, although both are holy and it is both of those things. Sex is the very wheel upon which the world turns. Consider the stang, placed in the witch's compass to act as Yggdrasil, the world tree. If the stang's branches call to mind Cernunnos's antlers, then in ritual reality, Cernunnos' very body serves as the fulcrum for all the realms.

The first point of the Iron Pentacle, a form of energy work practiced by Feri and Reclaiming witches, works from an expansive conception of sex. T. Thorn Coyle describes sex as "the power of the life force: lightning arcing down and earth rising to kiss it." She writes that "Sex is the rush of sap into the tree and down my legs. It is the caress of bee leg on rose petal, the rooting of the mole into the earth… Sex is connection to all life." [viii] As keeper of the mysteries of sex, Cernunnos is creation itself.

But creation is impossible without destruction, and here we see an aspect of Cernunnos not often celebrated by many of his followers: lord of death. As both hunter and hunted, Cernunnos liaises with the animals whose lives we take to feed ourselves; as the god who dies on Samhain, he creates space for his own rebirth. The serpent so often seen in his hand points us to the generative *sprawl* of the land and the snake's ability to shed its skin and renew itself. Thus does Cernunnos serve as a god of cycles and impermanence, turning the wheel of the year by rutting and dying, rutting and dying. *Hoof and horn, hoof and horn, all that dies shall be reborn.*

I never thought of Cernunnos as a god of water before my peculiar dream about the river. Traditionally, fishermen have left offerings to the Bucca on the seashore, but Gary expresses skepticism that this practice reflects an authentic relationship with the deity. [ix] Other connections to water are so scant that they seem scarcely worth mentioning. After my dream, I puzzled over the image of Cernunnos the ferryman; meanwhile, my career aspirations and sense of identity crumbled to dust and I was forced to construct something new from the rubble. I performed a strange card reading in which Cernunnos insisted that I was "free." Then, at a moment that felt precisely timed, I happened upon a footnote to one of Robert Cochrane's letters to Joseph Wilson, founder of the 1734 tradition:

In some versions of the myth [of the Castle of the Rose, or the abode of the High Goddess], [the castle] is on an island surrounded by the River Styx. The soul crosses over...by paying the ferryman (*the God*) to row them across the misty waters in his death barge (emphasis mine). [x]

Cernunnos serves as the witch's guide, leading them through spiritual death and rebirth to wisdom, illumination, and power. True initiation is not simply admittance to this or that tradition; it is a process of utter destruction and recreation. Has Cernunnos torn you down, ripped you apart, devoured you and reshaped you into something stronger and wiser? He will if you ask it of him. This is his fearsome and loving gift to you, but he will not bestow it unless your trust in him is perfect and complete. And afterwards, you will find that the parts of you he put in the ground—the parts you thought were so integral to your sense of self—were the parts that had already rotted.

#

I am lying in bed a few months after my ferryman dream, performing my nightly card reading before going to sleep. I ask an inconsequential question; it is answered; I prepare to put the cards to bed. Something behind me begins to tap the wall.

I tense. In Los Angeles, earthquakes are a constant threat, and I wait to see if I must rush to protect my child in the next room. But nothing is shaking. Rather, the tapping behind me, strong and insistent, sounds like someone knocking.

Lately I have had frequent visions of Cernunnos rattling the knob of my door, wanting to be let in. I cut the deck and finger the top card, alert but unafraid. "Who's there?" I whisper. The card I turn over is the Devil.

#

In a way, we are oddly lucky, in this historical moment, that Cernunnos's most frightening aspect—vehemently suppressed and denied by an entire generation of witches—has thrown off his shackles and is rising to prominence again. As late capitalism ravishes the earth and Evangelical Christianity completes its transition into a vehicle for unchecked racism and violence, witches reconsider our relationship with our wild god. Is Cernunnos really the docile and harmless spirit that the architects of mainstream neopaganism would have us believe? Should we really muzzle ourselves in order to build bridges with the people who lock children in freezing cages? No, we say, and step into our power. Although it is more useful to think of the Devil as a composite or even a class of deities rather than one discrete personality, our god of the wildwood and teacher at the crossroads is indeed everything our opponents hate and fear: a catalyst for our instinctual selves and freedom from the Church's control. As the world burns around us, the stag god demands that we see him in his entirety. *I am not harmless*, he whispers, and *neither are you.*

"For the 'old style' witch, the Devil is the initiator and awakener of power, vision and wisdom, and the revealer of the witch's path," writes Gary; what we now call the Devil is "that which deviates from the restrictive and normative ways of 'civilized' folk."[xi] Peter Grey puts it thusly: "The Devil is a sign that She [the Goddess] is also here, as the path into the hidden wood the Devil indicates and down which the witch must walk."[xii] As one of the deities our people call "devil," Cernunnos pulls us over the stile and through the hedge so that we can draw magic from the untamed lands of our deeper, wilder selves.

But be warned: this magic must be used to liberate, to serve the earth, to grow into our full capacity as human beings. If we attempt to use this magic for solipsistic fantasy—if we turn it into the nepenthe of "positive vibes" or use it to manifest more fodder for our ravenous egos—then it will promptly vanish, leaving us to plummet over a precipice of our own making. The witch god has no interest in such games.

#

Tonight is a night to aspect, to invite my beloved into myself and serve as his vessel. In my hands I hold a snakeskin, symbol of regeneration, and a handful of coins, symbol of wealth. I open my channels to him and feel him pour into me. The wildwood shivers and unfurls within me. No words come—in the 23 years I've served him, Cernunnos has never once communicated with me through speech—but he takes hold of my limbs, sees through my eyes, and fills my compass with his power. The working is a success.

Some encounters with Cernunnos are formal, ritualized affairs. Others are spontaneous. Even here in the city, where car engines roar and the topsoil has been scraped away, I find him in the tenacious dandelion, the sidewalks cracked by tree roots, the precarious hummingbird nest. In any tucked-away wild place, in any hidden hedge, there he is.

#

Beaten down by poverty wages, medicated with enforced consumerism and the addictive light of screens, we have been brutally tamed. We bow our heads as our forests burn and our ecosystems collapse. We swallow our anger as the wealth we create is hoarded and our children are gunned down. Our howls die in our throats when those in power tell us the only remedy is more of the same. We will never rise up; we are doomed.

Or so we are told to think.

Cernunnos's ascension has not occurred in a vacuum; our yearning for the wildwood is a response to the forcible disenchantment of our world. Perhaps Cernunnos's crown of illumination is growing, branching, arcing toward the stars as we rise up to defend our land and ourselves. Perhaps the specter of the witch is no mere disruption to the gears of capitalist patriarchy, but its endgame.

When Cernunnos shows himself to you, when he reveals his infinite and beautiful complexity, will you rise to meet him? Will you accept his trials and seek his hidden light? Will you shudder and retreat into the safety of the mechanized world? Or will you walk the path of the witch?

[i] Nicholaj de Mattos Frisvold, *Craft of the Untamed*, (Oxford: Mandrake, 2011), 34-36.

[ii] Ibid, 36.

[iii] Kate West, "Cernunnos Chants and Songs," Paganspace.net, last modified July 15, 2009, http://www.paganspace.net/group/thecernunnoscorner/forum/topics/cer-nunnos-chants-and-songs.

[iv] Raven Grimassi, *Old World Witchcraft: Ancient Ways for Modern Days,* (San Francisco: Weiser, 2011), 192.

[v] Here I pause, apprehensive of the backlash this statement may receive. A literalist contingent of practitioners has, in recent years, worked hard to stamp out syncretism and monism among witches and pagans. Outside of Internet orthodoxy, however, ordinary pellars and cunning folk go about their business, approaching the gods in whatever form the gods appear to them. It is worth noting that, although Cernunnos is generally considered a male god, Bucca is androgyne; however, it is also healthy to remember that sex and gender have never been hard and fast polarities.

[vi] Gemma Gary, T*raditional Witchcraft: A Cornish Book of Ways,* (London, Troy Books, 2008), 51.

[vii] Ibid, 58.

[viii] T. Thorn Coyle, *Evolutionary Witchcraft*, (New York: Tarcher, 2004), 120.

[ix] Gary, Traditional Witchcraft, 52.

[x] Robert Cochrane, Evan John Jones, and Michael Howard, The Robert Cochrane *Letters: An Insight into Modern Traditional Witchcraft,* (Milverton: Capall Bann, 2002), 48.

[xi] Gemma Gary, *The Devil's Dozen: Thirteen Craft Rites of the Old One,* (London: Troy Books, 2014), 10.

[xii] Peter Grey, *Apocalyptic Witchcraft,* (London: Bibliotheque Rouge, 2013), 81.

The horned God: Reflections from the hedge
Taryn Noelle Kloeden

He first came to me in the forest. I cannot tell you if I were awake or dreaming. At eight years old, I had not yet lost my child's wisdom. I knew the difference between dreams and reality was a matter of perspective. I remember the bright green sassafras leaves though, and the shadows of the oak trees. The being I'd come to know first as simply "Jack" stood at the tree line behind my house. It was springtime and he beckoned me outside.

My heart pounded as I took his green-tinged hand. I can't recall the first words he said—or if he said any words at all. I just remember the smile in his eyes where they peeked out behind his mask of leaves and how safe I felt running through the woods with him. Sometimes in our soft, walled worlds we confuse comfort with safety. There was nothing comfortable about the hours we spent digging in the mud, climbing trees, or stalking squirrels. I scraped my knees, soaked my socks, and exhausted my limbs. But I was safe, because in those moments with Jack I was exactly what I was meant to be: a wild creature.

In those early days, Jack appeared as a teenager with short pointed antlers nearly hidden by his leafy crown. He taught me how to creep silently over moss, and how to be patient enough to allow the forest animals to come to me. I talked to him every day, and though he did not always talk back or appear, I knew I was never abandoned.

But seasons change and we all change with him. As I moved into adolescence and the pressures of school, a social life, and growing up forced me out of my magical woods and into the "real world," Jack weaved in and out of my life—often popping up where I'd least expect him. He'd come to me in paintings glimpsed through shop windows, in book characters and movies.

I learned Jack had many names: Herne, the Horned God, Cernunnos, the list went on. But those were just myths, my brain insisted. Beautiful stories, but no more real than imaginary friends. I told myself such fantasies were in the past—fond memories of the childhood it was time to leave behind.

In my grown-up hubris, I sought to abandon Jack and everything he represented. I still loved the woods and the stories I acted out, but they became fiction—a hobby I loved, but no longer real" I split my soul in two. I locked the wild child away in a cage marked "imagination." I fed her scraps of whimsy now and again, but I dared not release her, lest she devour my hard-earned maturity.

But a soul divided cannot survive.

As a young woman pursuing a career in the sciences, my days were filled with textbooks, deadlines, and exams. But my nights were haunted. Night terrors plagued me, fueled by fear and disconnection. Even as I excelled—graduating summa cum laude from a top college, finding a job, starting graduate school—my heart was hollow. And in those dark, dusty ventricles echoed screams of inadequacy. Always at the core, a single question: why, why, why?

Why did I hurt for no reason? Why was I living the life I led? Why was I here at all? I didn't see it then, but those dark nights were the beginning of the shadow work that would lead me to a more authentic version of myself. But I couldn't get there alone.

When Jack entered my adult life, he'd changed. I usually heard his deep voice, guiding me, pushing me to marry the darkness in my soul, instead of exorcising it. When the Horned God appeared to me—be it in dreams, visions, or meditation—he'd become a man in his prime. Gone was the boyish youth and playmate. His horns had morphed into a rack of antlers and a full beard grew beneath his mask of leaves, though the laughter in his eyes gleamed mischievously as ever.

Together, Cernunnos—for that was the name I now knew him as—and I dove head-first into the apparent contradictions of my life. He showed me that my dual callings, as a scientist and a witch, were not in opposition. They were two sides of the same coin. He was God of new life and the Underworld. His existence proved there was nothing wrong with duality; there was, in truth, nothing more natural. I was right where I belonged, in the in-between.

Once I embraced my liminal nature, the path to healing became clear. I won't say it was easy. Nor will I tell you my journey is over. What I can say is that the Horned God continues to inspire and guide my steps along the hedge between the worlds of science and spirit. My work as an environmental scientist allows me to do my small part to protect the wild that raised me. My evolving craft as a hedgewitch answers that ever-present why. Life is worth living because of the change I can make, and because of the change this life makes in my soul.

Cernunnos gave me the key to my wild child's cage. He taught me it was safe to release her, to re-join him in the forests of my youth. Where once my heart had been empty and malnourished, it now beats hot with purpose. I am whole, a free creature of the wild wood once more. I am a child of the forest, a champion charged with its protection. For these truths, I have Cernunnos, my friend Jack, to thank.

I see the Horned God in every rising sun, reminding me that each day is a gift and a challenge to fulfill my purpose. I hear him in the wind rustling newly born leaves, and smell him in sun-drenched pine needles. I taste him in wild mulberries and hot, spiced wine. And every time I walk my hedge between realms and selves, I feel him walk beside me.

Finding the horned God in New England Roots
Kerry Purdy

I've been a devotee of a myriad of Celtic and Anglo-Saxon deities for a few years now, and the honoring of them has brought me quite a bit of joy and fulfillment. Digging deeper, I've found many individuals that have turned back to the "Old Ways" but still wish to honor the faiths that they were brought up in. We've all heard of "Christopagans" "Christwitches" and "Jewwitches."

What about me? I've always been aware of my fairly abundant New England roots-and fascinated by the culture and history. Yes, New England, as in the land of the Puritans. The rigid, somber, humorless Puritans-who were only responsible for the accusations of "witchcraft" towards tons of innocent individuals. No, they have virtually no excuses. Yes, they have quite a load to apologize for. And as I just said, that's quite a bit of my own background, so no one should get offended.

Truthfully, I'm totally honored to come from these people. As bad of a reputation Puritans do have, particularly in the Neo-Pagan community because of the witch trials, you can't help but be in awe of the courage and steadfastness of these people who risked everything to flee the British Isles to practice their faith without judgement on the untamed shores of New England.

So how did I find the Horned God in my own New England Puritan background? I mean, that's the last place that you would expect to find a glimpse of, not just a pagan god-but the very one that the Christians supposedly turned into "Satan"- the embodiment of all evil. I shouldn't. But I did.

The Puritans feared "the Devil" above all else. And they saw him as a literal figure-a horned man, just the same as the Horned God, Cernunnos, Herne. During the hysteria of the Salem Witch Trials, "witches" were literally accused of doing "the devil's work." I believe that at least one accuser insisted that they had seen a horned figure standing at the foot of their bed in the night. They believed that they had truly seen "the Devil."

I believe that they did indeed see or perceive something. But what was it truly? Yes, I do believe in a way it was what they perceived as "the Devil." And "the Devil" was really and truly the manifestation of fear. Fear of the unknown. Fear of what was different. Fear of…human nature?

The Puritans feared human nature. They feared *themselves*. The Church that they had established back in England to simply "purify" themselves from the Church of England, had turned into something else. A monstrous control system.

And the Horned God, Herne, Cernunnos, represents human nature. Primal human nature. He represents exactly what the Puritans feared. To the Puritans, human nature *was* the devil incarnate.

And this is where the Horned God comes into my life. This is how my own Puritan background played a part in me coming to discover Him.

When I picture Cernunnos, he's stepping out of the dark woods onto the wild shores of New England, and turning towards me with a look of joy on His face, at my people finally re- discovering Him. I say re-dis-covering because let's face it, the forebearers of the Puritans honored Him back in England for centuries before the church came into play. One would think he's an imposing figure, but he's not. To me, he almost represents an older brother figure. He wants to be my friend. He wants me to be free of fear, of restraints, much of which was probably passed down through my lineage from these people. And I know that I no longer have to let those aspects hold me back. I'm capable of anything.

Accepting such a deity means accepting yourself. And in a way, I believe that I have also put my Puritan forebearers to peace-and that's the first part towards freeing myself. There's no longer anything to fear.

Cemunnos - Encounter 1
SezzaJai Sykes

My passion lives in the woods. He is deep, far down, in the centre of the dark shadows. He grunts and bellows his calls out into the stillness. His breath is fecund and gives rise to the green moss and ivy curls. He leans his haunches on the Oak as they share the ages.

I come to him nightly, stealing and slipping into the forest, to feed him and be mated by him.

His hot seed surges through my veins turning me into light and stars. I see all of life. I sail through the web, I am lit up and grasp the nature of reality before I coalesce into golden nectar, dripping with dust spilling from my pores.

I slide into my skin, my cloak, and leave the green wood to return home at dawn.

I wash my face in the stream at the forest edge, whisper, 'I am coming home', then dance my way to my garden, singing.

hunter, Shifter
Emily Carter

For years there had been a horned figure in my meditations. In my dreams. The presence was distinctly male, but never clear, and always in the deepest, darkest depths of the forest. Not darkness as in evil, but darkness as in the heart of the forest, the heart of all things. He watched. He waited. He made himself known.

For years I largely ignored him. I had other Gods on my plate. Gods that, so the omens said, were not particularly in favor of me going to meet this horned man. So I did not. I did the work I was given, and was curious, but in truth I had no energy left to spare for the mystery. I started to hear the name, Cernunnos, and I wondered. But I did not seek. Somewhere in this span of time, I came upon a beautiful deer skull that spoke to me. It held power, and when I looked at it, the horned one in my meditations looked back. It came home with me, and I hung him on the wall, and wondered. But I still did not look.

Time passed, and the Morrigan came into my life. Her entrance upset things, turned the norm on its head, and started to rework my spiritual world. From what I now understand, that is not at all unusual. Her presence brought depth and breadth and upheaval to what had, for a time, become a narrowing of my spiritual life, a confinement that had started to chafe. I could breathe again, and it was wonderful. I had some freedom back. On Samhain, my life changed.

Six months later, it is Beltane. I have a ritual, mostly written by another. It calls on Cernunnos. I have a new ritual space. This is the first time it has ever been used. In the afternoon I go up, to the woods, to check on it. There is a deer waiting for me. It looks at me, I look at it, and then it turns and runs. Deer are not unusual, in these woods, but they surely are that close to the edge. There are two areas I typically see them, and the new ritual spot is neither. I try to take a picture, but my camera can't seem to focus on anything inside the grove. Everything is blurry. I head back down to the house, only to find it focuses fine down there. Hmm.

That night, I prepare. There is a storm gathering. I can feel it on my skin. I pick up the skull. Am I sure I really want to do this? The skull hums with energy. This night, Beltane, with a deer skull that hums and the storm overhead a hundred acres of forest. Is this truly a good idea? I do it anyway. The altar is setup. I light the torches for the walkway in and as I finish, lightning flashes overhead. It begins.

When I hail Cernunnos, things move in the woods. An owl calls, then another answers it. I feel eyes staring at me from the skull of the deer. Ancient, heavy. The presence is not what I expected. Gone is the calm, patient figure in the heart of the forest. In its place stands something tall and forceful, intense and implacable, and looking at me. The hunted, sometimes. But tonight… tonight I face the hunter.

I move on with the ritual, after making offerings to him and to others. When those are done, I return to the altar. Cernunnos is there, waiting for me. His presence hangs heavy in the air. I can see faint shapes moving in the darkness, outside the points of the circle. Some too tall to be deer, and not entirely here, and at least one of them with the sweep of antlers. I listen and wait. I watch the strange, wispy presences move on the other side of the elemental candles. I have the distinct feeling that stepping past that ring of fire would perhaps not be safe, on this of all nights. But the temptation remains.

Come, hunter...come and run with us.

I feel His call in my bones.

I listen to the animals, and feel the undeniable presence of the God who has answered my invitation. He has been waiting for me. That horned figure in my meditations, in my dreams. Waited years for me to call out, to answer, to see. For he is a hunter, and hunters know patience. The thunder rolls, the lightning flashes. For a time I lose myself in the night and the thunder and the lightning. It is a heady thing, the presence, the power, and the sheer wildness of it all raises the hair on the back of my neck. It speaks to my soul.

Hunter, shifter, come...

The words roll with the thunder.

But if I go to run in the woods, I may not return. And I still have Work to do, here. The urge, the call, is strong, wild, full of promise. I listen to an owl call once more. Another answers. Something moves deeper in the woods. I hear a few huffed breaths, something larger moving to my right, outside of the firelight's reach. The forest is alive all around me, and I revel in it. All too soon, it is time to go. Thanks given, rite ended, but still the presence remains. Not as obvious, now. The air no longer crackles with wildness and power, but as I put out the candles and the torches, I can feel his eyes. Only once his candle on the altar is put out, and the skull revealed by the harsh, artificial light of a headlamp, does it become simply a skull once more.

And I find myself wondering. What will it become when the sun sets tomorrow.

Cernunnos and Me
Woody Fox

My first meeting with Cernunnos was when I was 10, up in the woods with my dog when I'd at last been invited by the wood's faerie to enter their home. On the way to their hole in the ground they all stopped and started crying out in awe and wonder , things like "He's here, he's here!" and in the distance through the trees I could see a giant person approaching, the trees seeming to bow towards him and sparkling light everywhere, the woods becoming deafening with birdsong and that light shining brightly on his antlers. He spoke to them all , smiled at me and then he left as quietly as he's arrived. After spending the afternoon with the folk I went home, only to find anxious neighbours hurrying to me and freaked out parents as I'd been away for two days (so they said) I was a seer child and it had its great benefits, though it also could be a curse.

When as an adult I started 'working' with other witches I was already a devotee of the Goddess Danu vowing to protect her and all her creatures to the best of my ability. I was an animal liberation activist and a hunt saboteur and I found many kindred spirits in the Pagan world. My Pagan friends were mostly Gardnerian witches and it was here that I kept finding references and invocations to Cernunnos, the great Hunter, the very, very hetero god, he that is the consort of the Goddess, the beast, the wild, violence, angry, 'our' god.

Often in the group rituals he'd appear and stand in circle and I'd find him looking at me, me the gay gu , the guy that has nothing to do with him, the guy who is 'taken' by Danu, the gay guy who believed the straight witches. In one group ritual, with 100 or so European witches he came over to me and said "you're mine" and I fled. That's when he started the hunt.

For a year he showed up everywhere, whether I was stone cold sober riding my bike through London's traffic, walking in the woods with my coven or sweating away in some pounding gay club he'd often appear, freaking me out.

The next Imbolc, in south London, my coven were doing a pathworking, going down in the earth and watching a seed start to open and when my seed opened. He was there. My shock was extreme and I tried to pull out of the trance but he held me there. "It's time" he said very gently. I rejected him outright saying I was Danu's but he wouldn't relent. When I came back into the room, there he was and I ran. Crossing London on the underground and busses running home and getting back to my flat.

There in the living room were Danu, Ceridwen, and Brigit - the triple Goddess that I worked with and there he was, sitting in the chair in the corner, legs crossed casually and smiling sardonically. I think I was crying by then, feeling released from the compulsion to race home only to find this scene in my 'safe' place of home.

Danu explained that I had to cross to his path then, become his devotee and as she passed the power over I felt like some stray mutt being pulled on a lead to its new owner. The initiation was then created, gone through and it was done.

Ok, it didn't feel that bad, in fact it felt pretty much like the connection I had to Danu just a lot wilder/chaotic/darker but I was fucking outraged at him.

I'm a sulky sort of Piscean man and I hate having to do things I don't want to so I told him to f**k off and I refused to speak to him for at least three months, no matter where he appeared.

In month four I was in a park and he appeared sitting next to me, I didn't react but he didn't disappear either, just sat there, our backs against the oak when he started chatting very gently. Chatting like we were old friends and in some ways I guess we were. He reminded me about when I was 10, something I'd forgotten about, and asked how I was now with the 'sight', whether I could use it now or whether it was a burden like it had been back then. He felt so gentle, so caring, so kind and nothing like the raging God I'd expected. So we talked. I told him that I didn't want to be connected to a god like I'd had described to me all those years ago - the big butch hetero god when I couldn't connect to that or had any desire to.

He took me on a journey where he showed me himself and I was blown away by the enormity of what he was, the hunter and the hunted (though for food not for sick fun), how he cared as much for the rabbit as the human, how he was the god of the faerie races as well as everything else, how the wild was a terrifying place unless you had this Cernunnos link, when you could then plug in , so to speak, to the wonder of the wild and be a part of it. He showed himself mating with goddesses, with women, with men - mating was mating in his eyes, there was no one way.

So I got to understand things, the different way that he sees the planet, all life, the interactions between beings and mostly the need and urgency of protecting it all from the ravages of mankind.

So I became hooked. We started my whole witchcraft training again, from the basics to how I am now – still training after 30 years of becoming his devotee, it never ends, it's always going forward in joy of life and the wonder and mystery of it all.

Being a seer is fantastically handy now, healing, spelling and occasionally cursing with all the beings that I can communicate with, working Fae magics and elemental spells all with Cernunnos at my back. So my work with Cernunnos usually involves working also with the Faerie kingdom, spirits of trees, animals, other beings of the land, working with life and earth and all the parts in-between. Mostly the work we do is for the betterment of the planet though quite a lot of personal things too. My devotions most days are in song form to him, then he'll appear and we have a conversation.

I know I sound quite chummy with Cernunnos but I never forget he's a god. He often tells me things I have to do, the odd quest or time of a series of rituals- often for the benefit of myself – things about my health, what I should and shouldn't do – much to the amusement of my namesake Fox.

I do find him a jealous god – I'm not allowed to let other deities aspect me unless he says so and most rituals I do he wants to be there too (I'll often see him hiding in the trees if he hasn't been invoked!) He's often quite brutal in his demands though as a bit of a trickster too he can be bargained with (though you never get the better of him!)

But that's part of the contract between us. He helps me and I'm his priest, he gives me what I need and I do the work he calls for. It's a deeply beautiful arrangement and I will often find myself wondering how other humans cope without it!

So I'd advise people out there, don't believe what others tell you. Find out for yourself. Trust your allies, whether they are human or not and go on a voyage of discovery. Question the gods, the elements, the spirits and your fellow humans and find your own way to the wild, the sacred, the divine.

He told me a long time ago that the name for a priest of Cernunnos was a Herne, that that was what Herne the hunter was all those years ago, so here I stand, in my power, Woody Fox , a Herne of the great Lord of the Wild, Cernunnos!

Cernunnos and the Drum
Eva Leenknegt

I am not certain when I first met Cernunnos. I may well have encountered him in the forest before this tale starts.

Whichever the case, my journey with him started when I decided to make a drum. The first step of the process was a journey, a meeting with Cernunnos where we would ask for an animal that was willing to share its skin with us. Based on that meditation, we decided that deerskin would be best for my drum.

The philosophy of the person holding the workshop was to only work with wild skins that had been responsibly sourced (for instance, when a culling happens by rangers in a national park). He would start looking for that skin only after this initial meeting, and it would take however long it took. Essentially what that means is that, at the time of the meditation, the animal that was to become my drum was still alive. And so I was sent home with the task to connect to it in meditation over the coming days, to begin building up a relationship with it.

The next evening, as I sat down to meditate and closed my eyes, immediately I experienced a strong sense of presence. A voice echoed through my head, saying:

'You are asking me for an animal's life.
What are you prepared to give me in return?

There he was, the lord of the hunt, pointing out to me the realities of life and death, the relationship between hunter and hunted, and the need for balance. I could get that drum if I wanted it, but I would have to pay for it. Naive as I was at the time, I agreed to compensate him for this. But as I was to find out after that: lives are expensive...

After that first meeting, more encounters followed. In my meditations, he took the shape of a shaman-like figure, surrounded by a group of hunters. He gave me tasks to help me better understand the meaning of death, and helped me establish a stronger connection to that deer. I was still waiting for him to name his price though...

Then, one night, towards the end of a meditation, when I was already preparing to finish up for the night, something unexpected happened. That time, I was to be the prey: I found myself surrounded by the hunters. One of them took his knife and slit open my skin, which then turned into some kind of bag containing a spirit-version of me. They helped me to step out of the bag. One of the hunters folded up the bag-skin and handed it to me. Then Cernunnos spoke.

I want you to give me your own skin in compensation.
I shall ask you to become my drum.

I asked if I could think about it for a while (I didn't want to make promises that I would regret later). I took a few days, but eventually decided to take the risk, returned to the meditation and handed my skin over to Cernunnos.

Soon after that, I got a message that a deerskin had been found, and if I would maybe be available at Samhain for the drum-making workshop? (This was an individual one-on-one workshop, with no other participants.) It is only in reflecting back on the experience now that I realize that this timing cannot possibly have been mere coincidence.

So I made the drum. After that, not much happened initially. I had held a public ritual at Samhain, the day after the workshop, in honour of Cernunnos, hoping that with that I would have paid back at least some of my debt. A few other request to hold rituals followed later on, so I sort of assumed that that would be it: that he would occasionally be calling on me for that kind of task.

I didn't hear much from him during the year that followed. Once, at Imbolc, he told me to let him know '*when I was ready to take things to a deeper level*'. A call which I ignored at that time. The druid course I was taking had me immersed into rather intense shadow work, so I wasn't exactly available to take on extra work. It seems that he respected that, for the time being. (In retrospect: probably because that was work which he would have required me to do anyway...)

However, once I had finished that course, his calls started becoming more insistent, and so eventually I asked if he expected me to be his priestess. The reply came immediately: *'I want you to make an oath to me at Samhain. You can write it yourself, but be aware that I will take you up on your word. Whatever you decide to offer, I will take.'* Effectively, he had given me a two month deadline to decide how much I thought my skin was worth...

I had read quite a few warnings online about being careful what promises you make to the gods, and so I took plenty of time making lists of what I would be ok with and what I considered to be impossible. Kind of like how you would go about setting down a contract of employment, setting down the rights and duties of employer and employee.

It is only in retrospect that I am recognizing his hand in a lot of the things that happened next. For it would turn out that a business contract was not really the kind of oath he wanted from me: I began to be showered with smaller and bigger hints about the deeper meaning of marriage, and the way in which husband and wife vow to mutually support each other.

The more I thought about that oath, the more I realized that the right way to go about this would be to model it on a marriage vow, where the basic statement is essentially: I care about the causes that are important to you, and I am willing to enter into a partnership with you. I will trust you with my life.

Which cause was this? A very deep love for the forest and the trees. And so, if I made a vow to Cernunnos, that vow was at the same time a vow to the forest. An agreement that from that moment onwards, I would consider the forest to be my kin and my family, with all the obligations that come with that.

That is what I wrote in my vow: from this moment onwards, I will be yours. I agree to serve as your Voice, and to dedicate my talents to your causes. Till death do us part. As a formal sign of confirmation, when I spoke those words in my dedication ritual, I took a cord and used it to bind a piece of tree-branch to my wrist.

A day or so after the ritual, I did some divination to see where things stood. A single card jumped out: The empress. Together with a soft whisper. 'Congratulations on your marriage. You are my wife now'.

I was more than a little bit flabbergasted at this point, but in retrospect: what else should I have expected? If I list all the signs, then there is no escaping the conclusion that he had asked me to marry him. Upon which I wrote marriage vows, and performed a handfasting ceremony – all without being aware of the deeper significance of these actions.

Trying to understand what had happened, I began to look up and read everything I could find on spirit marriages. I found that in certain traditions, it was quite a common way for a shaman to be called into service that way: their main spirit ally would appear to them and ask them to marry them.

I would like to stress once again that this is not a kind of relationship I ever consciously sought out. In fact, I am still struggling to understand what it even means, especially since I have no real-life points-of references to fall back on: my sexual orientation is asexual – which is essentially a natural form of celibacy: the most important people in my life have always been friends rather than romantic lovers (in fact, you could and can quite easily provoke me into a rant of how undervalued friendship often seems to be in our society when compared to 'real love'). I have never felt like I missed out on anything. I was, for all intents and purposes, a happy single.

Yet now suddenly I found myself in a relationship with a god who made it quite clear that what he had in mind for us was a relationship that included a romantic aspect, something which was completely uncharted territory for me.

He did teach me how to understand and explore the needs and reactions of my own body. (Independent of orientation, anyone can get sexually aroused given the right kind of triggers. I have not and will never feel sexually attracted to another human being. But I do now sometimes feel arousal when I sense Cernunnos to be near...). That experience was very healing for me because it allowed me to stop feeling like I was an alien (a feeling brought about by the nagging fact that there was a huge part of being human, namely everything to do with sexuality, that I completely failed to understand, because it was so completely outside of my own realm of understanding). I will forever be grateful to him for giving me that.

The fact that I am still struggling with mightily however, is seeing him as a life partner in the emotional sense. I've been used to taking my own decisions and being emotionally independent for so long, that it is hard to allow someone else to be part of that, even if (or maybe because?) that someone else is a deity.

I wouldn't want anyone to have the impression that this is simply a tale of a god who decided to fall in love with a human girl.

The depth of my spiritual experiences started to increase enormously from the moment I took that vow. As if someone had opened gateways in my mind that had previously been closed... Like being dropped in the middle of the ocean and told to swim, when you'd never even seen anything wetter than a glass of water before.. Experiences of spirit possession have pretty much become a daily routine, and I suddenly gained the ability to receive messages from gods and spirits through automatic writing. (Where beforehand I would be very satisfied if I managed to catch even the slightest glimpse of a spirit guide in meditation...)

And I can tell you that, even with a god on your support team, this is a mighty struggle: suddenly studying every bit of magical theory that I can get my hands on, is no longer a matter of curiosity, but of necessity. For there are an enormous number of dangerous errors one can make when suddenly finding themselves in the middle of the big wilderness that is the spirit world. I have made quite a few of them so far, and every day is another learning experience.

Of course these gifts were not given to me for mere entertainment. The work I am being called to do for Him is to act as a voice for the forest, not in the sense of activism against forestry, but on a spiritual level: connecting to the trees, learning what lessons they have to teach us, and sharing what I have learned with other people, so they may come to know the forest in a different way – as a never-ending source of wonder and wisdom. And hopefully a side-effect of that will be that people will come to understand the true value of a forest, and just how much trees deserve our love and protection.

Cernunnos and the Green Man
Rev. Christopher Wallace

Cernunnos first stared at me through the stone eyes of a Green Man carved into a cathedral I was researching. As a Catholic clergyperson, I was naturally curious as to why such a relief could be found in so many areas of Christian worship. Upon learning more about his many archetypal references across various cultures, I opted to delve deeper. What began as pure academic inquiry ultimately evolved into a personal journey to experience this multifaceted deity. Born and bred into a monotheistic tradition that conceptualized "God" as eternally perfect, benevolent, and unchanging, the concept of a god who could be imperfect, capricious, bounteous one minute and harsh the next, intrigued me. His own likeness to the human condition endeared him to me and, quite honestly, ameliorated my own private misgivings regarding the same in myself.

We recognize that the same water which precipitates tsunamis can also spend eons gently carving out canyons in rock face. I believe it was this latter approach that the Horned One employed to slowly shift my awareness of him from purely archetypal to something more profound. As I came to terms with the primal nature of Cernunnos, I could feel him inviting me... no... daring me... to peer through his eyes. That particular dynamic was, and occasionally continues to be, a learning curve replete with moments of both unease and amusement.

When the inexperienced roams the wooded path of The Hunter long enough, awareness inevitably flourishes. Background noises developed into subtle whispers; whispers grew into tentative conversations. Now, many turns of the wheel later, I consider myself privileged when discerning his existent voice in the cry of the wild hawk, the instinctive imperative of the rut, and the elemental storms that periodically visit the Gatherings where I join with my fellow Druids in honoring his name around a fire. The chiseled stonework eyes I once dispassionately observed are indeed alive and watching us with both warm joviality and a sincere warning: don't stare too deeply unless you intend to join The Hunt.

Cernunnos and Manannan: Journey Through Fire
Sarah Bernard

It was early August 2018, fires were burning all around Northern California and Southern Oregon. I had begun my trip while the Carr fire was raging in Redding and only 45% contained. Two other fires burned south of there near Winters and Ukiah. I witnessed falling ash at Shasta Lake and heavy smoke that required masks to exist comfortably outside near the town of Mt. Shasta. The mountain was shrouded in smoke and hard to see from town, while on a clear day the mountain is seen rising high above this quaint little place. Orange sunsets and hazy skies every day. It looked like the apocalypse. I was camping and living outdoors for the next two weeks, but these fires were not going to stop me from this much needed trip I take every year, the trip of personal transformation.

North of the Klondike and Taylor complex fires, which had merged the evening I was in Gold Hill, I was engulfed in smoke so heavy it woke me up choking. After 4 days of sleeping in a tent with smoke all around I found myself in Oregon. I was at the third site for the trip, a primitive campsite next to a stream that flowed out to the Pacific Ocean. Nestled in deep woods, surrounded by old growth redwoods, the giant trees provided shade and cool fresh air that I had been longing for since I had started the journey. Nature surrounded me. This place sang to my soul and brought me peace.

I had just picked up a bottle of whiskey at Rogue Distillery in the town of Newport nearby. I had yet to pop the bottle to enjoy some of this delicious drink. But I had other plans for the first pour, a calling to do some workings. I decided on an impromptu offering to Manannan and Cernunnos to send healing rains and new life to the areas damaged by the fires. I kept it simple. Just my voice, my intention and this bottle of whiskey.

I asked for healing of the land, water to quench the parched soils, for new life to spring up and restore the beauty, but also not hide the destruction, as the scars should be a reminder that we humans need to be more vigilant of our actions on our mother earth. I asked for the rains to move south and help those putting their lives on the line, to stop the fire and to protect the innocents whose lives were threatened by these blazes, both human and creature of the forests. I poured the first serving from the bottle as an offering into the stream and onto the soil to both Cernunnos and Manannan.

I wrapped up and tucked in for the evening. I went about business as usual the next day and gave the workings the night before little to no thought.

The next evening, while settling into my tent for the night, I had an unexpected visitor to my campsite. I heard movement outside my tent. It became more prominent and clear. I knew this visitor was a deer; clear as day the hooved animal entered the campsite with a staccato like rhythm and stopped close enough to my tent that I could hear it's breath in the quiet night. I don't know why, but I said hello. I paused in silence and said it twice more. On the third hello, the creature outside of my tent took off through the bushes, making quite a ruckus as the sound of it faded into the forest. Silence again. I peeked outside, curious if I could see tracks. Nothing was visible. The ground was soft so there should have been something. Nevertheless my curiosity was satisfied, so I settled back into my tent and started reading again. Not long after that, I heard the familiar pitter patter of rain on the nylon fabric above my head. Then it all clicked. My offering was accepted. The working was starting. Cernunnos and Manannan responded, both in turn. The rain fell. On waking the next morning, I made a second offering as a thank you for the acknowledgement of my request. The rain fell for three days and it was beautiful.

This trip mirrors my personal journey. My life had changed drastically in the past year and the experience was like being reborn of ash and ember like the Phoenix. It was the catalyst that inspired me to focus on personal growth that had been stagnant for so long. I washed away my fears and pain in smoke, ash, rain and wind to become something new, stronger and whole.

Between the Mist and the Knife's Edge

Kay Bell

Cernunnos!

Lord of the wood, wild, and ancient wealth

Master of all beasts, space, and land

Liminal force between nature and man

Blessed with might! Blessed with health!

Forest lord, to you we feast, grace in hand

We walk your ways, praising in every span!

The first time Cernunnos made himself known to me was in the sharp inhale of a breath. It was the early nineties, and my family was on a road-trip to see my uncle in Florida. The drive was remarkably rainy all the way down with some despondent weather system moving through. It turned my child-mind to idle thinking through a car ride where my family flipped on Depeche Mode and Phil Collins, and otherwise expected peace and quiet.

We stopped at a tiny asphalt parking lot off a bend in the highway. Wandering off the black and yellow of the highway and parking lot, our feet crunched the rain-soaked gravel and wood-chip walkway. We headed toward an outlook that was almost invisible from the parking lot. Our walk took us around the trees, the way twisting around them in something like reverence. It seemed mystical and misplaced to my child mind.

My little heart pounded as I walked up to the stone outcropping, looking down to place my awkward feet. I was told to look up as I made a first step onto stone. My bright pink sandals made contact with the gray granite, and I found myself steeping into a different feeling of my own body. I inhaled the rolling fog, exiting my own sense of self and introduced to something impossibly wider and larger than myself.

The expanse of looming trees stretched before me. Each one barely could reach the height of the cliff's edge, but they all seemed to crowd my view. Soft shades of deep, dark green dressed the pines and Atlantic white cedars. A white, curling mist topped the trees and erased the horizon as the geosmin scents in the air bloomed with the just-passed rain. Forest and mist stretched as far as my eyes could see in any direction. The sun revealed its rays from behind the unfurling clouds, shining light on our view, but the mist was unyielding. The forest did not surrender its ponderous shadows.

Even more overwhelming than the view was the presence pounding in my mind. I had never known gender before in my life as something more than what someone else insisted on. In that moment, I felt male and far older. I felt wild, untamed, heaving in air as a stag would after running for miles. Never before had I thought of an antlered man, but I stepped into that presence: both as my sense of self, coming face to face with a being outside of myself, and as a stag overlooking the forest. I was in and part of His forest—all at once. My heart kept beating against my ribs and I felt the forest's pulse with me.

I felt right.

My thoughts solidified to being the antlered man overlooking the forest, bearded and arrayed in brown furs. I was fully myself in the liminal space between the life of the cliffside and the life of the trees below. I had no gender outside of this space, and in a breath of realization, I found that neither did He as a god that traveled every boundary. We were alive, and that was so much more than enough to understand who He was. I was in a perfect state between life and death. Life surged through me, with a potential death hanging over the ragged cliff-edge just a few feet away. That's what life was, He told me. I did not fully understand at the time. It's a difficult thing to be the observer and the one experiencing, especially when you're young. The knife-edge of always taking chances by just living was part of who He was. It was not something I had to attain or become. It simply was because I was alive and willing to listen. He radiated life and unity with the land, but just like the juncture between the branches yet to grow and the living tree, the horns yet to grow and the rack of antlers present in my mind, the knife-edge between life and death was where I could always find Him.

The mist rolled on, and the sun's rays melted into the expanse of fog.

I was the last of my family to leave that moment. I never wanted to leave. I momentarily picked up pine needles as I turned away, but felt wrong for trying to take something away from the place. I left them behind, and clambered into the familiar, prickly tan interior of that old black Honda. My mother voiced a small snippet about the place being discovered by an explorer somewhere up the family tree. To this day, I've tried finding that outlook online through various maps, and I've never rediscovered that outlook or any parking lot in the bend of that highway since.

I have found Cernunnos since: in a dome of storm-snapped pine branches in Tennessee, in planting fig trees in Texas, in hiking the freezing foothills of mountain ranges in the American West, and in handling the tendrils of new ivy growth. All of these experiences pulled me back to the rituals of the cycle of the year—crowning a continual relationship with the land and my god.

It was not just in the liminal junctures between mountain cliffs and cathedral-like forests that I found my god. It was in the liminality of civilization as well. Self-reflexive approaches to my beliefs helped me string together the many moments in which I could see His influence, and where it was not fully actualized or not Him at all. Reading through archaeology, folklore, and linguistics brought me closer, my mind running through data like the trees I once saw growing without count or number. In French, in Labarion, as a god of sky, earth, or neither, I have found His roots in Gaulish polytheism and brief hints of his being through the ancient European world.

A dream of another life uprooted my understanding of him and I used the knife-edge of my mind and the force of my spiritual being to understand Him again. In the dream, I lived in a world under His care and worshipped within my community. Again, I was male, with a wonderful wife and children. The dream raised many conflicting questions to my understanding of Cernunnos, and why such an experience of another life would be rendered if it weren't something I had already been through—or had just lived through. Was it right to experience a god in a manner at odds with all the reconstruction that I had assembled in my own practice? Was such an impactful experience just to be dismissed? How was I to come to terms with rituals and worship wildly different from the careful liturgies written for the cycles of the year?

With multiple degrees and a day job hell-bent on defining every variable and understanding each aspect of functionality under my governance, I resist the idea that I am not supposed to understand or comprehend a concept. My self-reflexive practice demands that I understand each system of thought and its appeal.

"Where is the boundary in that approach?" asks the Horned God to my puzzling and mental gnawing on an ever-larger bone. "Where does the liminality begin and end, leaving room for growth and a diversified mind?"

As I had to leave the outcropping to live my life, I determined that the mental stability my practice created was good and worth doing. It was also right to honor the experiences that I had lived through. If the trees in that early morning were truly without number, the fog forever overflowing, perhaps it was worth considering that my experiences of a god could be as well.

After all, all of life is mist, and we are only in it for a moment, tilted on the knife's edge. I intend to live in a manner that brings me closer to that wonder and sense of life I took into myself as a child. Between the rolling mist of spiritual experiences and the clarifying light of the mind, I will find the god of liminality again and again, until my body merges with the land for others to know and understand.

Part 3

Experiencing Cernunnos

The horned God and Autism

Kerry Purdy

I was diagnosed with an Autism Programming (I refuse to say "disorder") as a small child. In a world that still does not understand this neurotype, where many of these individuals, many of whom possess IQs of approximately 200, are still sadly dehumanized and underestimated, there is indeed much discouragement for so many of these people.

However, Autism could indeed have played an integral role in our ancient society. I don't remember where I read it, but it has been said that Autism may have evolved millennia ago in Europe, to give an advantage in hunting. If that is indeed true, think how essential these brains would have been in hunter-gatherer societies. It could be owed almost solely to Autism that our ancient ancestors didn't starve.

And this is where Cernunnos, being a god of nature and the hunt, comes into play. Could the Horned God come into the Autism community as a symbol of Autism? I can imagine that many of these individuals could very well have invoked Him before a hunt. He could have guided these brains and minds for thousands of years.

As a young teen, my parents sent me to a camp in the Blue Ridge Mountains of North Carolina that appeared out of the blue. The camp catered to Autistic and ADHD children and teens, and focused on wilderness adventures – backpacking, camping, and climbing. It was at this camp that I discovered my love of the outdoors. I ended up attending this camp for seven years, and to this day, thanks to them I'm an outdoorswoman – to the point where I am certified as a Search and Rescue Technician and a Wildland Firefighter.

I believe that this camp has helped people reconcile with what Autism truly is – and it's assisted many in accepting their neurotype, in a society where it is still greatly shunned.

Just the other day, I was sitting barefoot outdoors and I asked Cernunnos to give me a sign. I heard it instantly – the words STRONG, BRAVE BEAUTIFUL. I took these words as to what He sees me as. I believe that accepting Cernunnos is a metaphor for accepting a way of thinking that is still stigmatized in our society – and the first step in leading our society to accept it as well.

Autism is a way of thinking that has always been essential. Just as they could very well have played an integral part in ensuring that their tribe, clan, did not go hungry, in this day in age they are now, slowly but surely beginning to usher in the Cyber Age. In a world that is now completely and entirely dependent on technology – most of which was probably created by autistic brains – these are the best mindsets for cyber defense. These are, mark my words, the people that are going to end up having the last laugh.

Ancient hunters and twenty-first century cyber engineers may seem worlds apart. But they're not. They are the same brains, the same mindsets. Just as the autistics kept the people fed, they will end up saving the world if, and sadly when, the cyber catastrophe comes. Mark my words.

Invoke Cernunnos anytime you do something that requires autistic traits – physical strength, stamina, attention to detail and high intellect. A small invocation of your choice, a small offering, a song. Celtic music and black/gothic metal is a great invocation. I also have discovered that Cernunnos enjoys libations of chocolate milk. Whoever knew!

Even before you march off to a twenty-first century cyber war, where everything technical has shut down, crowds are rioting…the police and the military have been called in…and it's YOUR brain that can save the day…

Sit on the bare ground in nature if you can. Close your eyes, and imagine yourself, millennia ago, creeping through the wild, dark forests of Eurasia, spear in hand. Your sharp, focused mind sees the hoofprints on the ground – you can instantly identify what sort of deer it is. It is a great stag. Your sensitive ears can hear him foraging up ahead. You press on, your keen senses and attention to detail pressing you forward. Then you see Him – Cernunnos, the Horned One. Your hunt will be successful. Your life will be successful!

In conclusion, accept yourself, accept them – and vice versa. And by the way, neurotypicals can honor them too. They'll assist anyone – and long as they keep an open mind and a respectful attitude!

The Serpent's Call of Cernunnos

Ravn Thor

In the fall of 2014 I struggled with the life changing decision of taking hormones. I tried to live my life without such measures, but the fact of the matter was that even though my close friends affirmed and validated my identity as a man – I still could not recognize myself. The thought of starting testosterone scared me because I knew everything was going to change. I had this misconstrued narrative that something in me was going to die. For some transfolk that may be their narrative – "killing the man" or "killing the woman" in order to become their true selves. That narrative wasn't for me but it was in constant rumination.

I was driving across the Red River when I began to have a vision of a black snake shedding its skin. I consider this a vision because I had no context or reason to be daydreaming about a snake. It played like a movie in my mind and had a visceral sensation. When the snake completed its shed and revealed its beautiful shimmering opaline black scales I felt a deep sense of relief.

"The snake is still itself," was the thought that came to me. This was a revelation. I was like that snake – transitioning was like the shedding. I was not going to lose any essence of who I am – I was simply going to shed the layers that kept the truth hidden. The Truth that I am a man and the truth that I was going to die if I didn't start hormones. Transition is transformation and growth. It is the constant of being in between.

I started hormones the following year. In October 2016 I began having dreams and daydreams about a horned god calling to me. I wasn't involved in any magic circles or pagan groups at the time. I dabbled in tarot cards and was interested in new age stuff but I had no knowledge of paganism. Taken to the oracle that is the internet, I looked up "Horned

Gods," and to my astonishment there he was – Cernunnos. The one I saw in my dreams and daydreams. The pictures I saw of him sitting with animals… and holding a serpent. It wasn't until just recently that I realized my vision about the serpent was the one being held by Cernunnos. He called to me in that vision. I have a Facebook friend who is a High Priestess and I sent her a PM for some guidance. She told me the best place to make contact with him is in nature and if I see a buck I will definitely feel him. She explained that he is also a vital half of the life force, and that each person must follow their intuition to heed the call in whatever way is personal towards you, and not what you're told to believe.

"The best advice about Deity is to do what feels natural. It's nothing you can read in a book other than the stories themselves. Find the offerings that feel meaningful to you."

I took her advice and began my quest. I went on many nature walks, did nightly rituals and meditations. On my hikes I would see many young deer and bucks. I felt his presence intensely. My relationship with him is as mysterious as he is – for me there is a strong spiritual and psychosexual component. Because of dysphoria any sense of libido had been nonexistent, and so much of my work with this deity has been awakening my sexuality as a man – becoming comfortable and accepting of my body as is and letting go of any notion of lack. It is seeing myself completely undeniably masculine, and the presence of that phallic masculine energy radiates through me unencumbered.

When I made the decision to transition I desired guidance as to what kind of man I wanted to be – I found that through Cernunnos. To me he is the essence of sacred masculinity – mature masculinity – masculinity that is liberated from the chains of patriarchy. It is being sincere, assertive, and confident. It is being bold and courageous and sensitive and compassionate. It's expressing emotions in a healthy way and being proud of that expression. It is brawn and inner strength and poetry and song. It is unbridled and primal sensuality. It is raw passion.

It's healing the wounds from white supremacist patriarchal masculinity that tells men/masculine folx they can't have feelings, that they must constantly dominate others, that violence towards others or themselves is the only form of acceptable self-expression. It's a masculinity that does not need to "other" another in order to be complete. It is free from fragility. It is transforming that shame and anxiety into confidence and full humanity. It's embracing the divine from within and feeling proud of the transformation. This fully transcended masculinity is not threatened by the insecurity or empowerment of others. It is autonomous. By imprinting with Cernunnos I am open to receive whatever plans he has in store for me. When I want to feel and express his presence I do so by being confident, "Shoulders back and eye contact." "Be present, have presence," are among the quotes he has whispered to me.

I honor him by honoring myself. When I do my weekly testosterone injection I always do a small meditation and ritual. I hold it up as an offering and ask for his blessing. I place the syringe between two antlers on my altar and say something along the lines of, "may this bring me closer to my true form, may this bestow upon me the virility and vitality of your sacred masculinity."

I honor him by having self-respect and reverence for the natural world. Grooming and hair have become a deep part of honoring Cernunnos for me as a transgender man. The hair on my face and chest are the manifestations of the sacred masculine – they are signifiers of my becoming embodiment.

By working with Cernunnos it awakened many aspects that had been dormant – instinct and intuition. Instinct is an ancient knowledge – a primal knowing. Intuition is a feeling, foresight, and perception. Through Cernunnos I've balanced both. Following my intuition while trusting my instincts has led me to discover where I belong. In the past I had struggled with a sense of belonging anywhere. By following my instincts and trusting my intuition I became acquainted with a friend who was an organizer of a local Pagan group in town.

It wasn't until I went to Paganicon 2019 that I realized I felt the most visible, understood, and my true self in pagan spaces than I ever had in LGBTQ spaces. This is because my transition is enmeshed with my spiritual connection with the Horned God. By no longer denying my experiences with him, a whole new world of possibility has opened up – I have a solid community of people I can depend on and feel connected to. I have grown magickally and am becoming who I am meant to be.

During a powerful meditation I met with Cernunnos in the Sacred Groves. He whispered, "Becoming me becoming you, becoming you becoming me." Within that meditation and ritual we merged. Cernunnos is not just a deity, he is the Ideal Self I strive to be. He is my manhood ascending into the sacred masculine. If it wasn't for his serpent's call I would not be here. I hope my story can reach my trans brothers/sisters and nonbinary folx so that they can know Cernunnos is there for them too. Paganism can be focused in such a binary way (male/female), but there has always been space for people like us. When I first encountered Cernunnos he saw me for who I really am. His guidance has helped me become who I am now.

Lord of the Forests, God of the Green, may your blessings bestow upon those that read and heed your call.

Trans Cernunnos

Hana Russel

Cernunnos Devotion

Amara Firebird

I am a queer priestress of Cernunnos and I´d like to share the story of my devotion to Cernunnos with you.

Since I started my journey into spirituality and magic, Cernunnos, the horned one, the hunter, the stag in the wild woods was the archetype I most responded to. I worked with other deities (and still do), but always came back to them, even in novels I always was up to stories about mystery cults referring to some kind of horned deity.

A few years ago a part of my spiritual community and I went camping in the woods, somewhere in the middle of nothing, surrounded by fields and forests. A big bonfire burned day and night and chanting all night long drove away the idea of mundane life outside the camp. Something was different to the previous years, I felt uneasy, driven, watched. Felt soft moss under my bare feet, smelled the trees more intensely. And – most important – felt the urgent need to invoke Cernunnos, invite them into my body, being their vessel. I had the pleasure and blessing previously to carry diverse deities within me, but never Cernunnos before.

A dear friend of mine, an experienced and deeply spiritual priest offered me support and we made an appointment for later the day, trying to find a good spot in the woods for the ritual. By the time we met again he not only had searched for the very spot, but build a narrow path, made of fir branches, spiraling through the trees. It ended in a circle made of twigs and branches, a crone of oak leaves and fir waited in the middle of it.

We sat down and he asked me to tell him about my previous experiences with invocations and spiritual possession. My answer was accurate, detailed, overly intellectual, as I told him about my practice, my ways of getting into trance and what worked well before. After I ended my talk he said just a small sentence that hit me deep and shaped my spiritual work since then: I only work with yearning.

This resonated oh so deep within me. He told me to stand tall at the rim of the circle, skyclad, carrying the crone on my head. My gaze was soft as I glanced into the woods, hearing his voice in my back, seductive, warm and consecrating, praying to Cernunnos. I embraced the feeling, connected more and more with all that surrounded me, was nothing but mere longing.

And then Cernunnos was there. Everywhere, in me, around me, nothing else had any importance. This energy, this fierce energy rolled through me.

When I came back to consciousness I recognized that I had torn both my knees on the branches when I tumbled. It didn't matter. My skin sang, my blood rushed und I felt this energy in the root of my hair – and still do when I become silent and focus inwards.

Cernunnos is there. This was the very moment I decided wholeheartedly and fully aware to become a priestess of Cernunnos.

My friend burst in happy laughter, seeing the overly intellectual me lying there after a wild hunt – dirty, laughing, crying and panting. In the next hours my senses where sharp, I felt like I could hear very small movement in the woods and fields, see, hear, feel every critter and being and rushing into trance as soon as I hear a drum.

In the months ahead it became clearer which aspect of Cernunnos was most important for me – at least now. The transformation, the honoring and creating of rites of passages and transitions, to accompany creatures over thresholds. Part of my vow became part of my mundane life. I started to work as a professional speaker and ritual conductor, as a companion for milestones and try to raise awareness within the people to feel the need for processes of transformation.

Cernunnos is an aspect in every decision I make. Being there when I need encouragement and support, for instance when I am ill or need a surgery. I have a constant feeling of belonging, a deep connection and a clear devotion to Cernunnos, to my vow and to the requirements that come with the priesthood.

As a physical sign I wear a tattooed mask of a stag on my heart chakra, accompanied by a hare for life and a wolf for decay. Constant transformation.

A Mystical Meeting

Maxine Miller

A dear friend wanted to honor his Celtic heritage with a pen and ink drawing of his Scottish Clan Crest. His mates wanted t-shirts of the design, and so we found ourselves starting a small business. We began to make shirts for other Scottish Clans and were met with much success. It was fun, but I thought there was something missing. I posed the question to my business partner, "Is there anything in this Celtic vein that might be more artistically fulfilling?"

"You could draw Cernunnos," he said.

"Who?" I was about to meet my future in the form of the Horned God of the Celts.

I did a little research about Cernunnos. There was not a lot of solid historical facts to be found, but it didn't matter. Almost instantly he appeared to me with startling clarity. Every detail was specific, as if I'd known him in my unconscious mind all along. Excitedly, I got straight to work to capture this vision on to paper. I knew nothing about the Celtic Tradition, or Paganism in general, but I was about to dive in. A whole new world opened up to me – tales of great battles and poets, Gods and Goddesses, mystery and magick. In subsequent meditations, he appeared just as I'd first pictured him, except he was smeared with the blue paint of an ancient Celtic warrior. Being a true creature of the forest, he was powdered with dirt, nostrils flaring, and gleaming with sweat. He was powerful, feral, and charged with magnetic energy. In the vision, I bowed before him, overwhelmed and intimidated. He reached out an encouraging hand, and I took it without hesitation. I never looked back.

Some twenty years later, Cernunnos is still my touchstone and companion. I've depicted him with pen and ink drawings, watercolor paintings, and most recently, a statue. Because my bond with him is strong, I feel his pleasure in all my work, most of which is devoted to Celtic, Pagan, and magickal subjects. I am a lucky woman – Cernunnos whispers in my ear and I honor him in turn, now and forever.

Cernunno

Maxine Miller

Three-Card Cernunnos Monte

Rick de Yampert

My plane soared high above Ireland, returning me to the U.S. after 10 days of trekking around the Emerald Isle in search of what the Irish call "craic" – their term for "good times."

I also had come in search of "trad" music, the spirit of the poet William Butler Yeats, and the Sídhe – the Irish word for the "people of the fairy mounds," pronounced "shee," as in "banshee."

And I had journeyed to the land of my ancestors, during Beltane, the great Pagan return-of-summer festival, in search of Cernunnos – especially since my search for the antlered god of the ancient Celts had proved frustrating during my previous visit to Ireland 10 years earlier.

My second trip completed, my plane had departed Dublin and was high above Eire's patchwork of variously shaded green fields and hills. Scenes from my adventure flickered across my mind's eye like images spastically coughed up by some ancient kinetoscope: My ass-whomping tumble upon the Hill of Tara, which friend and fellow Pagan Gavin Bone would later attribute to the impish Sídhe. The "yahoo"-yelling thug-boys – Irish rednecks?! – who showered me with a cup of beer as their car sped by me during a country walk outside Galway. The eerie disquiet that descended upon me as I became lost in Slish Wood as sundown approached. Gut-twisting food poisoning in Sligo Town. My close encounter with that murder – *Oh my Goddess, a murder!* – in the heart of Sligo.

And Cernunnos.

What just happened? I thought, gobsmacked by all the turmoil and tragedy I had encountered across the Emerald Isle. And yet I felt strangely . . . *Alive. Renewed. REAWAKENED.*

As Ireland's green fields undulated below me, I was seduced into taking some photos from my window seat.

A last chance to capture the Goddess – and this land, the land itself, really IS the Goddess! I thought. *Maybe the Paps of Anu, those twin, breast-shaped mountains near Killarney, are below me right now. Ah Anu! Cormac's Glossary, that 10th century text, was surely right when he called you "the mother of the Gods of Ireland"!*

I began snapping the landscape below, which was intermittently, tantalizingly obscured by the tapestry of cumulus clouds just below plane level. My attention was absorbed by the land as I hoped to glimpse the green breasts of Anu, so that I hardly noticed the clouds dancing in the sky. I speed-shot several frames and quickly reviewed them on my digital camera's screen.

What the hell is THAT?!

In one frame a silvery, fuzzy but perfectly spherical object appeared, hovering in space above the clouds. My Rat-Prag Brain – my Rational-Pragmatic Brain – quickly chimed in: "Rick, my good man! That's a mere water droplet on the window, and your camera's optics somehow 'projected' its image out into space!"

I forwarded to the next frame. There was the spherical object, only it appeared to be further away – as if it had sped away perpendicular to my jet. A water droplet on the plane's window, I realized, would have appeared as the same size in each frame.

My Mysti-Intu Brain – Mystical-Intuitive Brain – spoke up, cooing in her sweet voice: "Rick, as Hamlet said, there are more things in heaven and earth than are dreamt of in Rat-Prag's philosophy! You just captured a UFO!"

I looked out the window. Nothing. Whatever it was, it had vanished as my plane had moved on. I smiled. Suddenly I felt like a character in

"The Mothman Prophecies," that 1975 chronicle of high weirdness – of UFOs and strange creatures and Men in Black and errant garudas – by supernatural investigator John Keel.

Well, the Sídhe are known as "the Shining Ones." And paranormal investigator Jacques Vallee explored "the parallel between fairy-faith and ufology" in his book "Passport to Magonia: On UFOs, Folklore and Parallel Worlds." So why wouldn't the Sídhe pop up into the sky in the shape of a fuzzy, perfect sphere to say goodbye to me? Or was that Cernunnos driving a flying sphere?! . . . What just happened?

Here's what happened:

I first visited Ireland in 1995. My family heritage is French and Irish, but unlike many who hail from the Emerald Isle, my family knew virtually zilch about our heritage on either side. People intrigued by my Irish roots would ask me "What county?" meaning which part of Ireland were "my people" from: Was I a Galway man. A Munster man? I would simply shrug and say, "I don't know."

So perhaps that explains why I didn't see my first trip to Ireland as a "return to my roots" thing. Instead I felt called to Eire to see – and feel – places associated with Yeats, whose poetry had touched my deep-heart's core and had a profound impact on my soul. I wanted to pub-crawl Dublin and hang out in places associated with U2, one of my favorite rock bands. I wanted to hear authentic, live Irish folk music, known as "Irish trad" (as in "traditional").

And, although I was new to my Pagan path, I felt summoned to see the Cernunnos on the standing stone near the Hill of Tara in the heart of Ireland.

But when does one begin the Pagan path?

As a child growing up in Los Alamos in the Jemez Mountains of northern New Mexico, I had felt a palpable, mystical connection to nature while climbing the nearby cliff ruins of the ancient Puebloan people – in a mountainous place called Tsankawi, as well as those ruins in Bandelier National Monument a few miles further away. (The term "Anasazi" is no longer used by historians to refer to the ancient cliff dwellers.)

Tsankawi was just five miles from my family's mobile home, and it attracted far fewer tourists than Bandelier. Standing atop Tsankawi's small mesa, it was easy and inevitable to slip into non-ordinary reality: The stony, ochre-colored earth was hard, harsh yet somehow welcoming – the deep grooves worn into the cliffs by the footfalls of the Puebloan people a thousand years earlier were testimony to that. The breeze atop Tsankawi would whisper-sing as it passed through the pinon trees. As a child standing under the massive expanse of turquoise sky and looking at the even higher Sangre de Cristo Mountains to the east near Santa Fe, I felt as if I were seeing all the way to the end of the world.

And the petroglyphs! Most notable, carved into a cliff face, was a boxy, three-foot human figure that my child eyes saw as a "carrot-top" guy, but the Tsankawi guidebook noted the plumes sprouting from the top of its head likely were corn husks or feathers.

Though I couldn't articulate it as a child, Tsankawi was the first place in space-time that I sensed Spirit with a capital "S." So, perhaps that was the beginning of my Pagan path – one destined to emerge then go dormant for three decades.

Never mind the huge contradiction of Los Alamos: Our mobile home park was a mere mile from the "Lab" – the very place were Robert Oppenheimer and other nuclear physicists developed the atomic bombs that were unleashed in World War II. Just down the mountain, the indigenous Native Americans had forged their existence for centuries amidst the awe-inspiring yet desolate beauty of the high desert terrain.

Ancient ones and A-bombs. Go figure.

Little did I know at that time that the Horned/Antlered God lay hidden in those cliff-dweller ruins and was watching me.

When I moved to coastal east-central Florida in 1990 during the early part of my newspaper journalism career, I wasn't startled to discover that my hikes through the swampy, gator-infested nature trails of my adopted home – the complete antithesis of New Mexico – nevertheless beckoned me with the same sense of unfettered wildness, a mysterious "other" that somehow seemed a part of me.

Images of the Green Man that I had encountered in books, and the "Robin of Sherwood" TV series with its portrayal of the demi-god Herne the Hunter resonated deeply with me. Then in some book on Celtic mythology, I "stumbled" across a photo of the Gundestrup Cauldron's Cernunnos.

Boom! I could feel etheric antlers sprouting out of my forehead as I stared at this … this alien, wild yet beatific Nature God that had finally revealed himself to me across 2,000 years of space-time. The scant historical record on Cernunnos and the unsolvable mysteries of the Gundestrup Cauldron – the god's Buddha-like pose, the Celtic motifs fashioned in Thracian style, its discovery in a Denmark bog – didn't diminish his appeal. Here was a being so at one with the Spirit of nature that he calmly holds a ram-horned serpent. He sits in the midst of a stag, boar, bulls, some sort of big feline and a boyish human riding a dolphin. His stag antlers perfectly mirror those of his stag companion – a creature which almost seems to be smiling.

A Brotherhood of the Forest.

I felt called to join that brotherhood.

This Cernunnos image led me back to books to re-explore those Green Man images carved into stone and wood across the British Isles and Western Europe. The Gundestrup Cernunnos led me to read about the 15,000-year-old, antlered "Sorcerer" painting in the Cave of the Trois-Frères in France – an image that still reverberates in my soul even though scholars recently have debated whether it truly has antlers and depicts a shamanic human.

The Gundestrup Cernunnos led me to the Cernunnos on the Pillar of the Boatmen from the first century C.E., and to the horned entities and horned deities of ancient cultures around the world . . . and to the Horned God of Wicca, Witchcraft and Neopaganism and . . . .

Oh my Goddess – I'm Pagan? Yes, I'm Pagan!

So began my Pagan journey, 30 years after feeling the winds atop Tsankawi blow through my soul. Then a few years after embarking on my Pagan path . . .

I will arise and go now, and go to Ireland . . . .

On my first trip to Ireland, I arrived a month after Beltane. A Gundestrup Cernunnos talisman, which I had found in a metaphysical shop back in Florida, dangled from a cord around my neck.

Truth be told, I was as spellbound by Yeats as I was by my new God. I had my guidebook and I was going to explore all the places in Dublin and especially County Sligo that were associated with the Irish poet: I was going to *see* the lake isle of Innisfree. Glencar Waterfall. Ben Bulben, the mesa mountain near Sligo Town that legend says has a "fairy door" through which the Sídhe pass into the world of humans. Knocknarea, a breast-shaped, mesa-like mountain to the west of Sligo Town and the place where legend says Maeve (also spelled Medb), an ancient Irish warrior queen and voracious seducer of men, is buried under the cairn (stone mound) at its top.

As these mythic sites hint at, Yeats and my burgeoning Pagan path were intertwined. Yeats's poetry, especially his early work, is informed by Celtic myths, a mystical connection to the land, and the liminal world of the Sídhe. He was an early and prominent member of the Hermetic Order of the Golden Dawn. He was fascinated by the occult and the spirit realm. He was quite pleased when, four days into his marriage to Georgie Hyde-Lees, she began to channel otherworldly beings through automatic writing, and he was afforded the opportunity to question them on all sorts of esoteric matters.

In "The Celtic Twilight," Yeats's collection of essays about Irish myth and fairy lore, he writes of the time he and a friend watched at night from seven miles away as a small light ascended Knocknarea: "I, who had often climbed the mountain, knew that no human footstep was so speedy."

I was ecstatic as I left Dublin in my rental car to head west to see Yeats Country, the 5,000-year-old passage tomb known as Newgrange, and the Cernunnos on a standing stone at the Hill of Tara.

Newgrange came first. I battled my claustrophobia and followed the tour guide through the narrow passage that led to the cave-like . . . make that the *womb-like* inner chamber of the earthen dome structure. In building this Neolithic temple that is older than Stonehenge and the Egyptian pyramids at Giza, the ancient Irish aligned its passage with the rising sun of the winter solstice – it is then that the phallic beam of the sun penetrates the womb of mother earth and the seed of the returning spring is planted.

The God mating with the Goddess. Spellbinding.

On to Tara.

Climbing the Hill of Tara in the heart of Ireland, I knew I wasn't merely walking the place where the High Kings of the ancient Emerald Isle were crowned. This also was a place inhabited by the Tuatha Dé Danann, the race of gods who settled in Ireland millennia ago. It's a place where the Sídhe have been known to cavort since time out of mind.

Tara is not a difficult climb – indeed, it's a hill that's only 300 feet at its highest point. But Tara revealed its majesty to me. Even from its modest summit, one can see for scores of miles across the rich, rolling, green-ribboned hills and plains of middle Ireland, and even glimpse the mountains of Galway miles away to the west.

Atop Tara are two earthworks composed of concentric rings with a middle mound in each, dating back to 2,500 BCE. One earthwork is known as the King's Seat (An Forradh in Gaelic) and the other is the House of Cormac. The concentric rings are no more than six to eight feet high, and the distant fields of Ireland disappeared and reappeared again as I trekked up, over, back down and across the two rings to make my way alone to the top of the mound of the King's Seat.

There atop An Forradh is the coronation stone of the ancient Celts – a pillar, about as tall as me, that's called Lia Fail, the "Stone of Destiny." Legend says the stone was brought there by the Tuatha Dé Danann thousands of years ago. Legend also says the stone will roar when touched by the rightful king of Ireland.

No roar, I thought as I tentatively ran my forefinger across the standing stone's curved top. I was a bit relieved since I didn't know what I'd do if destiny called upon me to be the High King of the Emerald Isle.

Atop Tara as I gazed across the heart of Ireland, I wondered if any of my Irish ancestors had ever walked this sacred place. I wondered if somehow their spirits knew that my spiritual path had led me to become Pagan, and that akin to them, I hold the earth and the sun and the moon and the stars and the forests and all of Nature as sacred, as evidence of a divine mystery that teems with not only a masculine energy – the Gods – but also a feminine energy – the Goddess.

I took my Cernunnos talisman – the most sacred of my spiritual fetishes – and gently touched the face of this antlered God of fertility, life and animals to the stony face of Lia Fail.

I made my way to the churchyard near the foot of Tara, where my guidebook said the Cernunnos sanding stone awaited me.

I saw a gray, sort of mossy, squat stone pillar about four feet high, but no sign of the antlered God of my ancestors. I looked around.

Maybe I'm in the wrong place.

No, this indeed was the stone.

Where's Cernunnos?

My heart hiccupped. My stomach felt like I had swallowed a carburetor.

Oh my Goddess, maybe the elements have eroded the image forever! Maybe I'm five years or 10 years too late. Or the Sídhe! They aren't trickster gods but they can be tricky and mischievous toward us humans. The bastards!

I stared at the pillar, then squinted at the pillar, hoping that a shift in my eye mechanics might summon the Antlered One.

Nothing.

I pondered if a shift in spiritual mechanics might conjure Cernunnos, but I was too discombobulated to focus on any such attempt.

I trudged away reluctantly, feeling like I had been duped while playing some sort of game of cosmic three-card monte.

Place your bets! Keep your eye on the Cernunnos stone as we, the Sídhe, mix the pillars up! Where's the God? Where's the Antlered One? Where's the King of the Beasts? You said where? There? You mean that one? Are you sure? That's the standing stone you wanna choose? Okaaaaay ... Nope! Sorry, you lose. No Cernunnos for you! Come back and play again any time. Oh, so you're from across the pond? Well, I'm sure one day you'll make it back to play Three-Card Cernunnos Monte again!

I walked to the nearby visitor center to check it out, and discovered a postcard of the Cernunnos stone.

There he is – the antlered God of my ancestors!

I wondered how the postcard photographer was able to capture an image of the pillar with Cernunnos so palpably prominent. Nowhere near as striking as the Gundestrup Cauldron certainly, but there he was – the oh-so evident antlers gave him away. The photographer apparently had used artificial lighting, cast at just the right angles, to conjure the Lord of the Animals out of the stone. Or perhaps the postcard maker had "cheated" even more and had doctored the image.

Sigh.

Back in the States, I developed my film and compared the two images: The great antlered God lived on the postcard. In my photo, he looked like a 3-year-old had mixed ochre clay and pig shit and slopped the glob onto the pillar.

Sigh.

***

Immediately upon touching down back home in Florida, I began plotting my return to the Emerald Isle.

OK, not entirely true: I began *dreaming* about my return to the land of my ancestors, Yeats, U2, the Sídhe and the pig-shit globby Cernunnos.

Ten years later – much longer than I had anticipated – I landed again in Dublin, Gundestrup Cernunnos talisman dangling around my neck. Beltane – May 1 – was only a few days away. I was eager to adventure across Ireland again.

As the N51 road skirted the River Boyne just past the Obelisk Bridge outside of Drogheda, I was hit by an impulse: *I will consecrate my Cernunnos in the waters of the Boyne!*

I was very near the site of the epic Battle of the Boyne, where in 1690 the forces of the protestant King William of Orange defeated the army of the deposed ruler, his Catholic uncle James II. But I was after different game – a quest other than immersion in history.

I parked my car by the side of the road, walked to the bank of the gentle Boyne, took off my Cernunnos and immersed him in the cool water.

This is strange, I thought. *Cernunnos is a forest god, a god in league with the animals of the wild woods, a god of the earthy realms – even if the Gundestrup Cauldron has that peculiar image of a boy riding a dolphin. Why am I dunking him in water? But it feels ... right.*

My trip to the west of Ireland, to explore Yeats Country once again, would take me by the Hill of Tara and its Cernunnos first. I was prepared for disappointment. As I left my car, my soul already was saying "Meh" as, with camera around my shoulder, I detoured from the path to the Lia Fail, the "Stone of Destiny," to first take a brief glimpse at the Cernunnos pillar.

And. There. He. Was!

Cernunnos!

Gone was the pig-shit glob of an image from my previous visit a decade ago. Instead, the Antlered One was announcing his presence with resolute glory: Antlers and face were readily discernible upon the gray stone. My Rat-Prag Brain, my Rational-Pragmatic Brain, sputtered and backfired, trying to make sense of this ... this revelation. But I was too astounded to rationally inventory possible explanations – intellectual ones or spiritual ones or otherwise – for this transformation.

No, this Irish Cernunnos was still not as resplendent as the one on the Gundestrup Cauldron, but my body felt like the Sídhe were bathing me in warm, electric honey. Here stood, for me, the most sacred object in all of Ireland: a Bronze-Age standing stone with a weathered image of Cernunnos.

I'm seeing the Cernunnos that my ancestors witnessed!

I took my Cernunnos talisman and oh-so gently brought it into communion with this stony, almost-vanished Cernunnos forged by some unknown craftsman in the land of my ancestors – an artist who also felt such a deep connection to the land and Nature and the lives of animals that it only seemed natural that a God should grow the antlers of a mighty stag.

After a few minutes – or was it a kalpa? I took photos.

I walked on air as I continued my journey to the top of Tara, to the two mounds known as the King's Seat and the House of Cormac. Though the physical size of Tara pales in comparison to the Jemez Mountains of my childhood in New Mexico, that day as I gazed across the fields of Ireland, I felt again as if I were seeing to the end of the world.

As I made my way back to my rental car, I slipped on the moist turf of one of the mounds and – whomp! – fell flat on my ass. I was unhurt and felt no pain, but the seat of my pants were caked in muddy soil. I laughed.

Getting back into my rental car, I tactfully changed into dry pants... and I realized my pentacle earring was missing – my Wiccan-Pagan star whose five points symbolize Earth, Air, Fire, Water and Spirit. My earring must have flown off when I fell.

I hastened back to the Hill of Tara and searched the ground where I had fallen. My pentacle was about the size of a dime, and I was about to concede it as my gift to this sacred site when I spied it among the blades of grass – now sanctified by the earth of this holy place.

Years later at the Florida Pagan Gathering, I would tell this tale to

Janet Farrar and Gavin Bone, two well-known Pagan elders, teachers and authors who, as it turned out, live not too far from Tara in the town of Kells in Ireland.

"Ah, that was the Good People playing a prank on you," Gavin said with an impish smile, using a euphemism for the Fairy Folk because, as anyone knows, you don't speak their proper name aloud because the Sídhe may see that as disrespectful – and one doesn't want to upset the Good People!

"They wanted your earring!" Gavin added.

More misadventures awaited me during my trek to the west of Ireland and Yeats Country.

In Slish Wood outside Sligo Town, I went on walk-about one late afternoon in the very forest where Yeats had trekked. An hour in, my gut began to feel like I had swallowed a dozen radioactive maggots when I realized . . . *I've lost the trail!*

Despite my experience hiking the mountains of New Mexico and the swamps of Florida, I had proved myself to be a tenderfoot in the land of my ancestors

I fought my rising panic as I picked my way blindly through brush and low-hanging tree limbs, telling myself to head toward the setting sun in the west. I thanked that good ol' Catholic St. Patrick for banishing the snakes from Ireland in case I ended up being stranded in Slish for the night.

I wonder if the Sídhe led me astray...

I finally stumbled back across the trail, after what seemed hours but must have been less than 45 minutes. My good fortune only reinforced the notion that the Sídhe had played a trick on me.

The next day in Sligo Town, I stopped at a metaphysical shop – I had found surprisingly few of them in Ireland – before heading to nearby Knocknarea. I once again would climb that mesa-like mountain and see if I might encounter the spirit of the lusty Maeve.

No Maeve, but as I drove back through Sligo to my B&B lodging, I was puzzled to see gardai (police) had cordoned off the street block that was home to the metaphysical shop. In the local paper the next morning, I discovered why: A man had been murdered there on the street during the time I was atop Knocknarea. The newspaper said the incident wasn't connected to any sort of IRA violence, but instead was the result of a long-running feud between two local families.

More misadventures – ones far less sad and tragic – awaited me. But those Irish redneck bastards who sloshed me with their Guinness, and the food poisoning that hammered me for several hours after eating at a Sligo restaurant, were easily tempered by my other, newfound mission in Ireland: to consecrate my Gundestrup Cernunnos talisman in as many sacred waters across the Emerald Isle as possible.

And so I did: In a stream trickling down the slopes of Ben Bulben. At Glencar waterfall. In Lough Gill surrounding the lake isle of Innisfree. The stream purring beside Thoor Ballylee, the 15th-century tower where Yeats had lived in the early 1900s. And, on Beltane itself, in the turlough at Coole Park. Indeed, all these waters were-are associated with Yeats, but that's only because the poet himself found his homeland to be filled with sacred sites.

My second Ireland adventure came to an end, but the adventure continued even in the air as that strange, fuzzy, flying sphere appeared outside my plane window.

Perhaps the Good People, the mischievous Sídhe, are telling me good-bye.

But that mystery was dwarfed by the realization that I had finally been able to say hello – face to face – to Cernunnos in the land of my ancestors.

***

Postscript: Some time after my return home, I was gleefully surprised to discover the goddess Boann in the book "Celtic Goddesses: Warriors, Virgins and Mothers" by Miranda Green. Boann, Green writes, is an ancient Irish fertility goddess and the "personification of the life-force of water."

Though there is no historical record, as far as I know, connecting Cernunnos and Boann, I couldn't help but think: *A-ha! Cernunnos, through the talisman dangling from my neck, had felt called to "mate" with Boann and her sacred waters across the Emerald Isle!*

***

Postscript two: Just recently a drummer friend showed me the new frame drum he had crafted. He had decorated the head with a curious image of a flute-playing coyote, inspired by a petroglyph carved into Mesa Prieta in northern New Mexico.

A Google search revealed that Mesa Prieta is home to some 6,000 petroglyphs, the largest such site in the state. Though I had never heard of it, the mesa is only 47 miles from Los Alamos, where I had grown up.

I ordered a book titled "Life on the Rocks: One Woman's Adventures in Petroglyph Preservation" by an artist and writer named Katherine Wells. In its pages I was stunned to discover Wells' drawings of some of the rock art created by the region's Puebloan people as far back as 1300 C.E. – petroglyphs that included numerous horned serpents.

Shades of Cernunnos!

The real-life sidewinder rattlesnake, which literally has horn-like protuberances above its eyes, no doubt inspired some of these petroglyphs. But one of Wells' drawings reproduces a 12-foot-long petroglyph of a snake with massive, longhorn-like horns. Wells' text said the image is Awanyu, a water deity of the ancient Tewa Pueblo people.

Even more stunning was Wells' drawing of a "magnificent life-sized upside-down horned human." Frankly, to me it resembles some type of space-traveling alien from a sci-fi B-movie. Its sphere-shaped head reminded me of – yes – the flying sphere I witnessed high above Ireland.

Still, more shades of Cernunnos!

In Irish mythology, Tir na nOg means "Land of Youth" and is the name of a paradise-like Otherworld.

Now my continuing quest to commune with the Antlered/Horned God of my Pagan path has taken a twist: I am being called to the land of *my* youth – to Tsankawi and Bandelier and the as-yet-unexplored Mesa Prieta.

I can only hope that when I set foot amidst the boulders and cliff faces animated by ancient carvings of animal flute players, carrot-topped beings, and horned serpents and humanoids, that Awanyu and that horned alien-like entity reveal themselves to me.

No Three-Card Awanyu Monte, please.

Part 4

Poetry

Song To Cernunnos

Jennifer Lawrence

Guardian of the wildwood,
You who watch over the creatures of the forest
and those humans who call the woods home,
I greet You each time my foot touches
the soft loam of the forest floor.

Hail to You, Cernunnos!
Antlered Lord, You who are guardian
of the shadowed shelter of rabbit and raccoon,
      fox and ferret,
      badger and bear,
      sow and squirrel.
I thank You for your watchful eyes,
I thank You for your fleet-footed step,
I thank You for your wisdom.

As the stag and the doe and the fawn
make their way under boughs of oak and alder and ash,
pine and fir, maple and willow,
You protect Your bourne with the
dedication of a father with his child.

You permit me entry to your domain,

And in gratitude I pour out libations to You

– wine and mead –

And leave offerings for You and Your kin.

Oats and honeycomb and dried fruit I set out,

Raw sugar and bread, apples and honeycomb,

And the prayer of these words,

> Composed in thanks,
>
> Written in thanks,
>
> Sung in thanks.

I pray You hear me, o Cernunnos,

With an understanding and acceptance,

And ask You that I may be welcome in Your realm

– the home of my soul –

For so long as I draw breath.

O Thou Betorqued Betined

Stephen Posch

O thou Betorqued Betined,

that sittest cross-legged

on the altar:

in thy broad lap, O lord,

I lay my prayer.

Cernunnos Lord of The Wild Woods

Amara Firebird

Cernunnos

Soul of the wild woods Keeper of secrets

You, who is carrying me to Liminal spaces

Jumping from stepping stone to stepping stone With swift feet and loving heart

Pushing me forward to jump through mirrors and veils Constantly changing perceptions.

In every border I feel you At seashores and cliffs

Where waves crashes onto stone and sand At the soft line of wood and land;

Where heaven and earth meet at the horizon.

There you are waiting for me, Eternal

Silent, joyful, divine Always changing But never fading

Cernunnos, pervade me I call upon you!

Wild hunt

Charlie Bondhus

i started compulsively collecting horns and horn shaped objects:

a cardboard replica

of a Viking helmet,

a twig shaped like antlers,

a shofar, a candelabrum, a cornucopia; i filled my meager home

with these and with many many paintings of goats and deer executed in
the american naïve style.

i still live in the city but now when i look out the window all i see is

brown	green
skin	horns
green	brown
horns	skin

beside the door I pile racks of hunting rifles belts of high velocity ammu-
nition,

crossbows nocked with fiberglass bolts, not because i want to kill you

but because you are the hunt and so i need to be that too.

Cernunnos Chant

Woody Fox

Cernunnos, Cernunnos,
He is new born fawn a leaping,
He is hawk come swooping down
He is sound of wildwoods talking
He is song of green and brown

Out the woods he comes a striding
From the hills and mountains high
See his antlers bright and bloody
See his hounds go hunting by

In spring he come budding
He brings life a flooding
In sun, life that's growing
All hail the horned god!
With leaves he is falling
with fruit he is sharing
With ice, life destroying
All hail the horned god!

Cernunnos, Cernunnos, Cernunnos, Cernunnos!

Autumnal Mist

Seviryn Hemlock

A silent wood, late autumns eve

Beneath bare, dirt laden feet the crackle on leaves

The trees quickly thinning, limbs going bare

Whispers of the past, ancient voices in the air

Heavy footprints treading o're the root and the brush

Under his footsteps, sticks and leaves, crush

Faster he approaches, not far behind

Your head full of fear, exploding the mind

In Autumnal fog, distorting, an otherworldly mist

The cracking of the forest, the branches a-twist

A scent of fermenting moss, with tall antlers like deer

Fear not, now, dear witch. Cernunnos is here.

Praise to Cernunnos

Creel Unbelove'd

Keeper of the Wilderness.

Protector of the Animals.

Defender of the Trees.

Standing in the shadows of the All-Tree,

Finger on the bowstring,

You give courage to those fighting

To keep their land and their water

From the Oppressors.

Holding the Torc of Truth-Speak,

You redistribute wealth

To those in direst need.

Skilled Tracker of pathways in this world

And those to the next,

Guide my steps.

Honored One,

Grant me knowledge and strength

To advance your just causes.

Horned One,

Accept my offering.

Hail, Cernunnos

Jean (Drum) Pagano

Hail, Cernunnos,

Lord in the Forest,

Everywhere I look

I see you there.

I see you in the streams that flow,

Tributaries, like antlers,

They carry water to the land.

I see you in still waters,

Branches, reflected from behind me,

Like antlers on my head.

Hail, Cernunnos,

Lord in the Forest,

Everywhere I look

I see you there.

I see you as I look to the sky,

Branches, like antlers,

Etched against the sky.

As the winds blow,

The antlers move through the Forest,
And in each case, you are there.

Hail, Cernunnos,
Lord in the Forest,
Everywhere I look
I see you there.

I see you in the trails,
As I walk deeper into the woods,
Antlers disguised as roots,
Look up as I pass by.
You are on this trail and the next,
The backbone of the Forest.

Hail, Cernunnos,
Lord in the Forest,
Everywhere I look
I see you there.

A swallow calls,
And the sound,
Slows down into a single tone,
It stops time as it lengthens
And holds.

Everywhere I look,

Cernunnos is part of the Forest.

In stream,

In sky,

In soil,

He becomes this Forest.

I feel him there.

Witch Lord of the Hunt

Ashley Dioses

In the great briar, the twisting brambles of twilight
Were decked with scarlet drops from thorn-pricked skin of youth.
They had to find the snow-white stag and then recite
A pledge of honor to the Witch Lord and His truth.

His mask was the eburnean skull of a stag,
With antlers reaching high toward the star-filled sky.
This form He did not show, for He'd make hunters brag;
He favored humble hunters, they allured his eye.

His eyes of smaragdine were blazing gems of will.
He was the Master of the Hunt, His will was law.
His furs were draped around Him, made from every kill.
His spear was stained with scarlet drops from flank and jaw.

The Witch Lord of the Hunt must grant a blessing for
A novice hunter to pass safely through His land.
No prey beneath His shelter, be it stag or boar,
Can fall without it, lest the hunter then be banned.

The Witch Lord takes great pleasure in just watching them
Investigate His woodlands, ever in the search
For Him in stag form, till at midnight they condemn
Themselves to sleep. He can depart then from His perch.

He smiles in thought and leaves them in their dream-filled sleep.
He wanders aimlessly throughout his woods till dawn,
For the arousing hunters would proceed in deep
Into His luscious forests, for His Hunt goes on.

I See You

Bill Murphy

My Lord Cernunnos:

I see You.

You Sir, are bold, but shy. Cernunnos, with a compelling gaze, peers at us through the branches, through the deep darkness of the forest. He stares at us, from the complexities of the roots of the sacred trees, the wells.

Cernunnos, where are You in history? There's no scripture, few pieces of art, and little scholarship. So where does your worship come from?

I did not need the Horned God.

I did not want the Lord of the Animals.

I tried to run from the Lord of the Wild Things.

No matter how fast and far I have run, You have tracked me.

When I close my eyes, what do I see?

I see you, Lord Cernunnos. I see you!!!

The God is silent.

Despite His quiet, He inspires my enthusiasm and dedication .

 Perhaps, silence is an integral part of His character.

Perhaps, He does not want to talk to me at this time.

Perhaps, the Giver of Gifts may share the boon of His speech on another day.

So I continue, spending my time in an amicable quiet in Your Presence. I will close my eyes, wait and listen for the sound of Your Voice.

Faithfully, I will bide my time, Lord Cernunnos. Until Tír na nÓg.

Part 5
Rituals

Cemunnos Ritual Pathworking

Ivo Domínguez, Jr.

Close your eyes and move inwards. Take a deep breath and become aware of any distractions from the outside world, (*pause*) sounds, sensations, thoughts and feelings that came with you to this ritual. Gather these distractions together (*pause*) and bid them depart until you return from this journey. (*pause*)

Open your eyes briefly and then close them again holding within yourself the image of where you are in the here and now. See a sparkling mist rolling, slowly filling your vision. See it grow thicker, and thicker, and thicker until you are enveloped in swirls of pearly mist, rosy mist, that glistens with sparkling motes. (*pause*) Although you are still, you feel motion all around you. Although you are still, you feel the fog swirling all around you.

The mist begins to thin and to lift up. As it thins you find that you are in a clearing within a great forest. It is late in the afternoon. Look around at the landscape. The sun's slanting light spreads honeyed light across the land. Smell the richness of the forest in the air and listen to the layered sounds of the wilderness. (*pause*) You notice that there is a faint path through the greenery. A faint path where the passage of feet, paws, and hooves have pushed aside enough of the plants so that you know where to walk. You take the path and hear the crunch of leaves and twigs with each step.

You walk, and the path leads to a greater clearing. You continue along the path and find yourself in a larger meadow. Again, you continue along the path and reach the edge of the forest. The path is clearer now, it has been smoothed by many feet. You look up and see that it leads towards a low hill with something glinting at the top of it. There are trees on the lower part of the hill, but the top is mostly rocky with patches of green.

You take the path towards the base of the hill. (*pause*) When you reach the hill you see that the path does not lead straight up the hill, but rather it spirals and turns up the sides to the top in a serpentine flow. You begin going up the hill. (*pause*) The wind begins to gust a bit and a twig falls directly in front of you. You bend down and pick it up. There are two oak leaves clinging to the twig spread apart in a manner that brings antlers to mind. You decide to take it with you as a token of the Wind's favor. With the token in hand you continue up the hill's turning path.

Finally, you reach the top of the hill. It is a gently rounded dome of granite and at its highest point there is a stone pillar the height of your chest. From where you stand, the setting sun looks as if it is sitting on the pillar. The sunset is painting the landscape with rosy hues and gilds the distant trees. Your skin begins to tingle, and you feel the air around you vibrating as if some massive presence was settling onto the hilltop. At that moment the sun seems to sink into the stone pillar at the crest of the hill. A startling silence descends upon you, so profound (*pause*) that for a moment you wonder if you have gone deaf. (*pause*) Then you look around and see that no blade of grass is stirring, the birds have paused in midair. (*pause*)

Time is holding still but you can still move, and you do. You walk up to the pillar and see that carved at its base is an indentation in the shape of the twig with the two antler shaped leaves. You place your twig into the indentation and a faint glow spreads over the surface of the pillar. (*pause*)

Time begins to move again, but with great speed as if to make up for its moment of rest. The sky is darkening, and the stars are blinking into visibility. A perfectly formed tree grows from the top of the pillar, racing skywards as if the seconds were years. (*pause*)

The Moon has risen and flown to the top of the sky directly above the stone pillar. The tree is reaching higher and higher. Its boughs reach the Moon and hold it in a wide armed embrace. (*pause*) Slender branches continue upwards reaching higher towards the stars. Your eyes follow the branches and then the tips of the highest twigs. There, there past the highest tip, there is a cluster of stars that trace out the shape of antlers, with two bright stars below them with the glow of eyes. It is one of the faces of Cernunnos... Horned One... the Stag God. (*pause*)

The wind rises, it rises! The wind whistles its way up the tree and shakes the branches. The branches sway across the starry face and the stars dissolve into a skein of light that spirals onto the branches of the tree. (*pause*) Twig by twig, (*pause*) branch by branch, bough by bough, and down the trunk, the tree begins to glow as if illuminated from within. (*pause*) Time speeds up once more and the Moon continues in its journey and the sky begins to pale.

You feel the first warm rays of sunrise touch your back. The sunrise touches the tree and it is transformed. For a moment it swirls with images of all of nature – the land, the sea, the sky and all its life. (*pause*)

Then as gently as night making room for the coming of day, the tree dissipates and is gone. The tree dissolves into swirling motes of light. You become aware again of the hilltop and the stone pillar.

A single jewel-like drop of dew has formed on the top of the pillar. You touch it with your finger and take the drop to your mouth. Taste it and experience it. (*pause*) (*pause*) Then take a deep breath. (*pause*)

The sense of thrumming presence has lifted. A warm Spring day is beginning with no more enchantment than that which is normal for any day. You bow to the pillar and begin your journey down the hill. As you spiral down the hill you encounter banks of fog where the sun has not reached or where the forest's shadows reach further. You walk slowly into the thickening fog. (*pause*) You decide to stand still until the fog lifts. You stop. Although you are still, you feel motion all around you. You feel the swirling and the turning all around you. Little by little, the fog lifts and you flutter your eyes open and find yourself back in the here and now. Back in the place where we began. Back in the place you held in your memory so that you could return.

Take a deep breath. Move your toes and fingers. Be here and in the now. Be here and in the now. And you are here!

Belotenes (The Feast of the Shining Fire)

Katelyn Willis

In May of 2016, I wrote this ritual to celebrate the spring High Day with the Grove of the Red Earth, a member grove of Ar nDraíocht Féin. In writing this ritual, I wanted to emphasize a few important aspects of Cernunnos as they related to my personal religious experiences with him. For me, Cernunnos was always a deity of liminality. He was one of the few gods I interacted with that existed in all three realms of the Celtic world: the Land, the Sky, and the Sea. He was simultaneously a god of wild places, a god of the dead, and a god of seasons. He was a god of crossroads. And, especially, for me, he was a god of transgressive gender.

A few notes on the ritual itself: this is a group ritual performed in the ADF style in a public grove setting. We used a live tree in my yard to represent the Tree Hallow, a fire pit to represent the Fire Hallow, and a cauldron filled with water to represent the Well Hallow. I taught the ritual attendees the processional dance, which they performed as I sang the opening song. We used three bells in three different tones for creating the sacred space. The bell with the highest tone corresponded to the Sky and the Shining Ones, the bell with the middle tone corresponded to the Land and the Wild Ones, and the bell with the lowest tone corresponded to the Sea and the Ancient Ones. I also worked with Steve Gwiríu Mórghnath Hansen, a Modern Gaulish language reconstructionist, to write the text for opening and closing the gates. I have provided both an International Phonetic Alphabet pronunciation for these phrases, as well as an approximate pronunciation using English words. However, it is perfectly reasonable to substitute English phrasing for these moments!

Opening the Rite

Statement of Purpose

We gather here in the in-between: a Feast of Shining Fire that marks the dawn of the lighter months. Rejoice! The dark days have ended! We eagerly await the fullness of Summer with a generous spirit, giving gifts to the Three Kindreds to ensure a bounty during the fruitful seasons. Let us sing and dance in tribute to Cernunnos, the God of the In-Between, who blesses us with fertile minds and fertile hearts!

Processional Circle Dance

1. Begin by placing your right hand on the left shoulder of the person to your right.

2. With your right foot, step one step to the right.

3. Cross your left foot behind your right foot and shift your weight on it.

4. With your right foot, step one step to the right.

5. Cross your left foot in front of your right foot and shift your weight on it.

6. Bring your right foot up next to your left foot and shift your weight onto it.

7. Lift your left knee up.

8. Place your left foot back down and shift your weight onto it.

9. Lift your right knee up.

10. Place your right knee back down and shift your weight onto it. You're ready to begin again with step 3 above!

Hymn/Chant

Rise up, O flame!

By thy light glowing

Bring to us knowledge, vision, and life.

Spring forth, O well!

By thy swift flowing

Bring to us healing, wisdom, and peace.

Root deep, O tree!

By thy slow growing

Bring to us courage, patience, and strength.

Creating the Sacred Space

Offering to the Outsiders

We gather here in this space

to encourage the good things of the world to grow and ripen and multiply

and to encourage the bad things of the world to wither away.

Kindred, if you are united with us in this goal, you are welcome here.

If you are not,

please take this gift and leave us be for now.

Likewise, let those of us gathered here prune from our own hearts and minds

the bad things that that may be growing there,

leaving room for new and good things to grow instead.

Honoring the Earth Mother

Earth Mother,

we seek kinship

with each other,

with the ancestors,

with the spirits of nature,

with the gods.

To find it, we must only look beneath our feet;

you are the thing which connects us all.

Guide us as we seek right relationship

with each other,

with the ancestors,

with the spirits of nature,

with the gods.

We honor you first because you are the source of all good things.

Honor us now with your abiding presence.

Invocation of the Spirits of Inspiration

We listen,

though we do not always hear.

We see,

though we do not always understand.

We do,

though we do not always comprehend.

Spirits of inspiration,

be with us now that we may hear,

understand,

comprehend.

Consecration of the Well

This bell belongs to the ancestors.

With it, I bless this well.

May its swirling waters reflect the currents of the Eternal Sea,

bringing us healing, wisdom, and peace.

Spirit of the Well,

be with us now.

Consecration of the Tree

This bell belongs to the spirits of nature.

With it, I bless this tree.

May its lofty branches reflect the branches of the Infinite Tree,

bringing us courage, patience, and strength.

Spirit of the Tree,

be with us now.

Consecration of the Fire

This bell belongs to the gods.

With it, I bless this fire.

May its leaping flames reflect the flames of the Boundless Sky,

bringing us knowledge, vision, and life.

Spirit of the Fire,

be with us now.

Opening the Gate

Invocation of the Gatekeeper (Elen of the Ways)

Elen,

Way-keeper,

Blessed one who guards the visible and hidden pathways that connect us,

who guides us in our journeys in this world and the one beyond,

come,

rest your feet with us for a while at this meeting place between worlds.

Slake your thirst,

sate your hunger,

and when you are through,

we ask that you carry these gifts and blessings

to whom they belong.

Opening the Well

With the power of flooding waters,

O bí in dhórath dhichórthu![1]

Opening the Tree

With the strength of mighty timber,

O bí in dhórath dhichórthu!

Opening the Fire

With the spirit of leaping flame,

O bí in dhórath dhichórthu!

Opening the Gates

Esi in dhórath dhichórthu![2]

Inviting the Three Kindreds

Inviting the Ancestors

Come drink with us, oh Ancient Ones,

in this hour of celebration.

Inviting the Nature Spirits

Come dance with us, oh Wild Ones,

in this hour of celebration.

Inviting the Gods

Come be with us, oh Shining Ones,

in this hour of celebration.

honoring Cernunnos

Invocation

Hail, Cernunnos, King of Beasts!

You walk in the spaces between;

You belong to nowhere

and also to everywhere;

Because of this,

you are the Walker Between Worlds,

and call all of the Realms Home.

As the Shepherd of the Dead,

we make offerings to you in the ancestral sea.

As the Green Man and as the Stag,

we make offerings to you in the wild places.

As the God who marks the passing of the seasons,

we make offerings to you in the shining fire.

In this moment,

be with us,

that we may thank you for your blessings.

Offerings

Traditional Grove Offerings

Offering to Selu, the Goddess of the Green Corn, who was once honored here

Offering to Frigg, Patron Goddess of the Grove, who strengthens our magic

Offering to the Kings and Queens of the Pantheons honored in our grove

Personal Praise Offerings (x3)

Prayer of Sacrifice

We have made our offerings;

we have prayed our prayers.

Elen,

Wayfarer,

these are the gifts and prayers we ask you to deliver.

Carry them now to where they belong.

Reading the Omen (Ogham or Tarot)

Have our offerings pleased you, o Cernunnos?

What blessings do you bestow upon us?

Are there any messages you wish to tell us?

The Cup of Blessing

Calling for the Blessing

Cernunnos,

let your blessings pass into this cup,

that we may drink from it and be blessed by you.

Hallowing the Cup

Behold, the cup that contains the waters of life!

With the blessing of Cernunnos and all the Kindreds gathered here,

this cup is hallowed.

May it heal us, inspire us, and transform us.

Affirming the Blessing

A gift of the Kindreds for the people who belong to them.

Returning the Waters to the Earth

Thanksgiving and Farewells

Thanking Cernunnos

Cernunnos,

In this briefest of moments,

you belonged here;

You belonged with us,

and we belonged with you.

But the woods are calling,

and we know it is time for you to return to them.

We thank you for your presence;

we thank you for your blessings.

You are welcome to return and feast with us

whenever the paths lead you here.

Thanking the Gods

Shining Ones,

we felt your presence with us

and we thank you for it.

You are welcome here always.

Thanking the Nature Spirits

Wild Ones,

we heard you dancing with us

and we thank you for it.

You are welcome here always.

Thanking the Ancestors

Ancient Ones,

you shared our cup with us

and we thank you for it.

You are welcome here always.

Closing the Gates

Deconsecrating the Fire

For a moment,

this fire was not just a fire,

but the fire of the heavens.

Now, it is once again just a flame,

burning quietly.

O bí in dhórath inchórthu![3]

Deconsecrating the Tree

For a moment,

this tree was not just a tree,

but the tree that reaches between the worlds.

Now, it is once again just a tree,

growing quietly.

O bí in dhórath inchórthu!

Deconsecrating the Well

For a moment,

this water was not just water,

but the well of ancestors.

Now, it is once again just water,

pooling quietly.

O bí in dhórath inchórthu!

Closing the Gates

Esi in dhórath inchórthu![4]

Thanking the Gatekeeper

Elen,

you have carried our messages across the realms.

You have done your duty to us,

and we thank you.

You are welcome here always.

Thanking the Spirits of Inspiration

Spirits of inspiration,

you have served us well.

We thank you for opening our ears,

clearing our vision,

and guiding our actions.

You are welcome here always.

Thanking the Earth Mother

Earth Mother,

you have grounded us during this rite.

We thank you for your goodness

and for your abiding presence.

You are welcome here always.

Closing the Rite

Let us go now,

filled with the spirit of generosity,

and bestow our own blessings upon the world outside our circle.

[1] [o bi ɪn ðorɑθ ðɪxorθʊ] (Oh be in though wrath the whoreth who) = May the gate be opened.

[2] [ɛsi ɪn ðorɑθ ðɪxorθʊ] (Essie in though wrath the whoreth who) = The gate is open.

[3] [o bi ɪn ðorɑθ ɪnxorθʊ] (Oh be in though wrath in whoreth who) = May the gate be closed.

[4] [ɛsi ɪn ðorɑθ ɪnxorθʊ] (Essie in though wrath in whoreth who) = The gate is closed.

Epilogue

Into the Future

Jason Mankey

There are some who view the gods of pagan antiquity as beings stuck in amber. For those individuals, the gods of the pagan past are exactly the same today as they were 2000 years ago. A careful reading of history easily disproves that sort of thinking: deities well attested to in the historical record were always changing. Over the centuries gods both gained and lost attributes, changed appearances and geographic realms of influence, and often times gods even merged with one another. Over the course of forty-plus years I've changed a great deal. The deities many of us work with have existed for millennia and will continue to exist long after we are gone, think of all the changes that might happen in that length of time!

When it comes to change, adaptation, and transformation I can think of no better example than Cernunnos. Though we don't know a great deal about how exactly Cernunnos was worshipped in the ancient world, we do know that Cernunnos is honored very differently in 2022 than he was in the year 22 CE. Two thousand years ago there were no Wiccan circles for Cernunnos to show up in, and while there were Druids 2000 years ago, modern Druids most likely do things very differently than their forebearers. And yet, as these pages have proven, Cernunnos continues to be with us, adapting to the circumstances of the present day.

As someone who has written extensively about the modern Pagan Horned God, there's a part of me that always cringes when Cernunnos is conflated with the Greek God Pan, but should I be cringing? Perhaps Cernunnos himself has chosen to absorb some of the attributes of deities like Pan? I don't think the presence of today's Horned God (and with that Horned God, Cernunnos) in our circles and in our lives is an accident. We human beings are devastating the planet, and we need a conduit to connect with a natural world so much greater than ourselves: why not Cernunnos?

It's possible that there are more worshippers of Cernunnos now than ever before. We have no idea of just how widespread C's worship was in the Ancient World, but today he's inescapable wherever Druids, Polytheists, Witches, and Pagans gather. In 2000 years archeologists will be digging up statues of Cernunnos on six of seven continents and will find thousands of paintings and drawings of the gods we all love so much. Cernunnos is very much present in today's world and shows up in our world in a variety of roles (as suggested by the contents of this very book).

While working on this anthology I was also working on a book dedicated to the idea of the "bigger" Horned God as found in Modern Pagan and Witchcraft traditions.[1] During my research for that book I stumbled upon something I had previously missed: a female horned figure contemporary with Cernunnos and also in Gaul. Like Cernunnos, this figure carries things symbolic of wealth, in most instances a cornucopia. Could this be a female Cernunnos? A spouse? A daughter?

The identity of this female horned (they aren't quite antlers) figure will never be known, but I can't help but think she's another way to enter in the mysteries of our beloved god. In the Ancient World there were often several different versions of the same deity, still the same figure but often unique to a particular area or attribute. Today we have Cernunnos Denton, why not also Cernunnos Horned God and Cernunnos Femelle? I know there will be some upset by that last epithet, but it seems likely that deities operate differently than you or I do. Besides, whatever draws someone closer to Cernunnos is fine by me (and John).

There are lots of different Cernunnos in this book, and yet at the heart of it there's also only one Cernunnos. The antlered god revered in these pages likely served several different roles for the Gauls, and he does the same for us today. In the coming years and decades those roles will only expand. In my practice Cernunnos is the "Witch God" in the tradition of Paul Huson and others; the figure I call to when working magick at my altar. But to me Cernunnos is also the Lord of the Wild Spaces and the protector of the Sacredness of Nature. At Samhain he stands between this world and the next as

1 That book is "The Horned God of the Witches: and was published by Llewellyn in 2021.

the Dread Lord of Shadows, connecting me to those I've lost in this lifetime.

When talking to other devotees of Cernunnos, one thing I'm always struck by is how much I see of the god I know in the descriptions of him by others. Maybe they don't honor him as a god of the dead, and perhaps they honor him in a Druid space instead of a Wiccan one, but there's always a thread there that connects their experiences to mine. That thread is why John and I wanted to put together this anthology. That thread is what unites all the different experiences in this book. May that thread continue to grow.

hail Cernunnos.

Printed in Great Britain
by Amazon